MOTHER EARTH'S
VEGETARIAN
FEASTS

Other books by Joel Rapp

Mother Earth's Hassle-Free Vegetable Cookbook
Dear Mother Earth
Grow with Your Plants the Mother Earth Hassle-Free Way
Mother Earth's Hassle-Free Indoor Plant Book

MOTHER EARTH'S VEGETARIAN FEASTS

by
Joel Rapp

illustrations by
Marvin Rubin

WILLIAM MORROW AND COMPANY, INC.

New York   1984

Library of Congress Cataloging in Publication Data

Rapp, Joel.
  Mother Earth's vegetarian feasts.

  Includes index.
  1. Vegetarian cookery.   I. Title.
TX392.R36   1984   641.5′636   83-13111
ISBN 0-688-02213-8

Printed in the United States of America

First Edition

1 2 3 4 5 6 7 8 9 10

BOOK DESIGN BY MARIA EPES

For Lynn and Don and Sam and Emma

Contents

MOTHER EARTH'S
VEGETARIAN
FEASTS

Sharing My Discoveries

❧ Hello again!

In our last culinary adventure, *Mother Earth's Hassle-Free Vegetable Cookbook*, I explained why I, Mr. Mother Earth, the Plant Man, had turned my attention to vegetable cookery: "So that those of you who want to start eating more meatless meals but are afraid, as I used to be, that vegetable cooking is dull, or a lesson in self-denial, or too difficult, or whatever, can be assured that it is indeed none of the above. So you can discover, as I did, that eliminating meat from your diet, or at least cutting way down, will *not* mean the end of epicurean feasting. *Au contraire!* You will, in fact, find you'll be eating better, enjoying it more, and spending less. I'm sure you'll discover, as I did, that a well-planned, carefully prepared vegetable diet will not only not be the end of your gourmet experience, but will be the beginning!"

Well, I hope that prophecy has come true for you. It certainly has for me! Over the past four years my understanding and appreciation of food and cooking have risen to the point where vegetable cookery—once an experiment, then a gratifying hobby—has grown into one of my truly passionate loves. Whereas before I was probably best described as a gifted amateur when it came to food and cooking, I now think I've reached a stage where I could, at worst, be described as Gourmet, Junior Grade. (Gourmet, by the way, meaning a person with a great love of food and cooking, is interchangeable with epicure and gastronome, while gourmand usually means someone who's a glutton. . . .)

This growth has come as a result of my moving to New York City, arguably the most food-aware metropolis in the land, and of my natural curiosity and desire to expand and take on more exciting culinary challenges. As a radio talk-show host I have had the opportunity to interview and learn from dozens of great chefs, restaurant owners, food critics, and cookbook authors, and have come to realize that a good cookbook can, in its own special way, be as much fun to read as a good mystery or romance—a wonderfully satisfying experience as the author describes, mouth-wateringly, the pleasures and joys to be found in individual foods and recipes you can taste and smell and can't wait to try. My new vantage point in Gastronomical Heights (overlooking beautiful Vegetable Valley) has come also as a result of devouring food magazines, not to mention the countless articles about cooking that appear almost hourly in practically every magazine and newspaper; and finally, my arrival at this most exciting epicurean plateau is due in huge measure to Miss Page, about whom I shall speak more in a moment.

Having reached this plateau, I now want to share my discoveries with you. As once I was known as "The Missionary of the Green" because of my zealous preoccupation with recruiting people into the Houseplant experience, now let the greens be vegetables instead of philodendrons! Brothers and sisters, spread your culinary wings, follow my flight-plan, and soar upward into new, more sophisticated, headier heights! Hallelujah!

No, you're probably not going to find an absolutely-brand-new-never-tried-before recipe in this book. Ever since Ms. N'Og, a Paleozoic cave-maker, accidentally dropped an onion into the dinosaur stew, scratched the combination onto her wall, and excused the indelible graffiti to Mr. N'Og by calling it a recipe, people have been carving out cookbooks. There are literally thousands of tomes on the subject, each overflowing with recipes for soups, salads, main dishes, desserts, ad infinitum—and each and every recipe is most surely an adaptation of one that went before.

But so what? Sure, there are only just so many vegetables and herbs and spices available in even your most exotic markets, even as there are just so many musical notes, or story plots, or paint colors—but there are myriad subtle ways to mix and match and blend and bake so that although a hundred recipes may look almost exactly alike on the printed page, a dash of this or a soupçon of that—not to mention the unique touch

There are literally thousands of recipes.

of the cook who's preparing it—can make one person's Russian Vegetable Pie a rousing *"Da!"* and the other's a baleful *"Nyet."*

After considering the thousands of possibilities, I've chosen these vegetarian delights to illustrate to you that vegetable cookery can be every bit as much an art as that practiced in any kitchen of the world! In these pages you'll find dozens of menus, some literally from soup to nuts (well, at least to a dessert topped with Peanut Butter Sauce!), all of which contain recipes that call for ingredients available and at their best and most economical during the season I suggest they be prepared. If cooking is more an art than a science—and I believe it is—it's difficult to come up with many absolute rules for ensuring truly great cuisine. But one rule that's pretty close to universally accepted is—with the occasional exception of, for instance, using canned tomatoes or even canned pineapple in cooking—ALWAYS USE THE VERY FINEST AND FRESHEST INGREDIENTS AVAILABLE. And that means shopping carefully for fruits and vegetables in season and at their peak.

It won't take you long to realize that most of the menus in this book more properly should be called feasts, or at least banquets. In real life, on a day to day basis, none of us—least of all me—eats the kind of meals I've put together for you. In the first place I couldn't afford it, in the second place only professional chefs at the most expensive restaurants cook like this every night and I don't ever want to lose my amateur standing, and in the third place eating dinners such as these any more than once a week would probably qualify you as a gourmand and definitely qualify you as overweight.

But certainly, every once in a while, it's perfectly okay to damn the torpedoes and go full speed ahead to treat yourself and your special guests to as many exotic, rich, delicious taste treats as you can find the time and energy to prepare. At a fine restaurant, given the chance to taste everything on the menu (just a little taste), you'd do it, wouldn't you? I would—at least I'd try everything that sounded good. Same thing at a buffet— you know you always load up your plate with far more than you'd ever eat under ordinary circumstances, but it's fun, isn't it?

So if any of these menus looks as if it's too rich, or too bountiful, or whatever, either drop something from the menu,

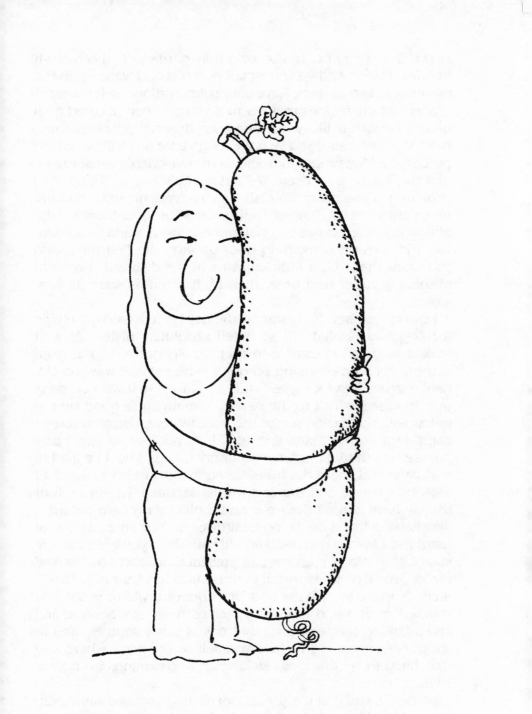

Always use the finest ingredients available.

switch the gooey dessert to colorfully garnished, sliced fresh fruit, or—best of all—serve small portions and wake up in the morning to two or three days of absolutely glorious leftovers!

Some of the recipes may seem a bit more complicated than others. More than likely that's because they are. Just read them carefully, make sure you've got enough time and will be able to purchase all the proper ingredients (or reasonable substitutes), and you'll always succeed. Well, *almost* always . . . Things can go wrong in preparing any dish—an inadvertent addition of too much spice, or the "wrong" spice, the subsequent, often fatal attempts to correct the original mistake, overcooking, too thin, too thick—but if something does go awry the first time, and you know that with a little adjustment the dish will come out absolutely super next time, then try it again as soon as possible.

I can remember, for instance, the day I discovered the recipe for Eggplant Roulade. It sounded absolutely divine. Alas, it looked next to impossible to prepare without a degree from some chic French cooking school. I stared at it. It was too elegant to make just for myself and I was afraid to invite company over in case it stuck to the pan or something (a good rule to follow with any recipe you're the least bit tentative about), so I compromised: I'd make it, and if it turned out as good as I guessed it would, I'd call a few hungry friends who'd be glad to rush over and share the fruits (or eggplants) of my labor. So I took the plunge and the result was dazzling! The lucky four friends have spread the word and, hoist by my own petard, I now have to trot it out by request three or four times a year, at least. But I love to do it, and so will you. Once you get your first standing ovation for an elegant presentation, you'll be hooked for life. You'll be transported to those twin Nirvanas of Nourishment, Vegetable Valhalla and Herb Heaven, where you'll find yourself mixing and matching recipes from this book, using and adapting recipes from hundreds of other sources, and finally, even inventing recipes yourself to the point where you may have to be dragged, kicking and screaming, from your kitchen.

I promise you that the process of getting involved with cooking and food is one of the most joyful and exciting adventures you'll ever have.

Things can go wrong in preparing any dish.

Peeling the Walnuts

❧ I have to tell you about Miss Page.

Marian Page Cuddy is her whole name, and although ours is not a storybook romance—rather, it's a cookbook romance since I lost my heart while she was editing *Mother Earth's Hassle-Free Vegetable Cookbook*—it's certainly not half-baked because we've lived happily ever after ever since.

I have to tell you about Miss Page not only because her love and understanding have changed my life but, almost as important, also because her vast and glorious knowledge of food and cooking has been an inspiration. Literally!

Probably the quintessential example of her attitude and influence occurred the night she decided to make Linguine al Pesto. To you, that might not sound like such a big deal, but to a certified pesto freak such as I it sets off a rush roughly equivalent to making your point with a grand on the pass line, an evening with Oscar Peterson at Carnegie Hall, and a Dr. J. dunk shot all rolled into one. Now there are some things you can prove mathematically and other things that more aptly qualify as "judgment calls," but the fact that Miss Page makes the world's greatest Pesto Sauce falls somewhere in between: I know it, but I can't prove it, if you get my drift. And I, my friend, besides being the definitive pesto freak, am also the definitive expert on Pesto Sauce. It's amazing how someone who didn't even know what Pesto Sauce was until a few years ago, can become an expert so fast. Call it a gift, call me an idiot savant, but when it comes to judging Pesto Sauce my talents are legendary and much sought after, and when it comes to making Pesto Sauce, Miss Page's gifts transcend legend into the stratospheric realm of culinary miracles.

Like very few other things in life, there's no such thing as bad pesto. It's just that some is better than others and, no matter how you serve it, Miss Page's Pesto is the best of them all. If I were one of those hoity-toity restaurant critics, I'd describe it like this: "The Linguine al Pesto à la Cuddy was perfection itself. The pungent basil was underlined with the slightly heavier flavor of coriander, the garlic subtle but readily discernible. The classic marriage of Parmesan and Romano became a euphoric romance, and then, suddenly, an electric surprise!—not only the expected texture of the pignoli, but the additional crispness of what I suspected to be walnuts."

Anyway, I sat in the kitchen trying not to salivate overtly as Miss Page bustled about. The olive oil, garlic, and fresh basil leaves were loaded into the blender (only fresh basil will do, and lots of it), the Parmesan and Romano were waiting to be introduced, and then Miss Page turned and handed me a bowl filled with big, brown, wet hunks of shelled walnuts.

"Here," she said. "Peel these."

I blinked, then flashed on a Mae West movie in which Mae offhandedly instructed her maid, "Beulah, peel me a grape."

I laughed. "Sorry," I said. "I thought for a minute you'd asked me to peel these walnuts. . . ."

"You heard right. They have to be peeled."

I looked at her, bewildered. "They do?"

"Of course," she said. "That little layer of brown skin is bitter, and—" She stopped and smiled down at me pityingly. "Trust me on this one, okay? If you want it perfect, you've got to peel the walnuts."

She went back to her tasks and I fell to mine. I suppose because peeling walnuts is mindless work at best, I began to drift off into 1960s altered-consciousness thoughts as I sat there laboriously scraping the thin layer of skin off each individual walnut, leaving behind a shiny, ivory-colored piece of nutmeat.

I started to think about how this is what *great* cooking is all about. This is the kind of loving care the truly masterful chefs must exercise to create the dishes served to royalty, or at the Four Seasons. This is why a meal at certain restaurants can cost three to four hundred dollars for two. The difference between good food and four-star cuisine was that simple—in the latter, you always "peeled the walnuts"!

Fifteen minutes later I took my first bite of Miss Page's Pesto.

Magnificent; better, if possible, than any pesto she'd ever made before. If the truth be known, it was perfect.

"You know," I said, "there's a lesson to be learned here." I took another bite, then looked at her with a beatific smile on my face, the kind you allow yourself after a revelation. "I mean, peeling walnuts is about more than just making pesto. It's about life. In any field—business, athletics, arts, whatever— the people who are willing to take the time to peel the walnuts are the people who will always come out on top. The champions!"

She grinned because she loves me. "Heav-vy," she said, then nodded toward my plate. "Now shut up and eat."

I fell to. I could revel in this Pesto alone with my thoughts, and besides, it's not nice to talk with your mouth full.

Okay. Thanks for allowing me to share that story with you. Now let's get into the kitchen.

By the way: There aren't any recipes in this book where you have to peel the walnuts.

Unless you want to.

An All-Vegetable Company Dinner

೭ It's Wednesday afternoon. Saturday night—just hours away—the Boss or some VIPs are coming to dinner and this is one meal that's got to be more than good. It's got to be memorable!

Your mind begins to whirl. You start to think about those dazzling menus—complete with absolutely to-die-over color photographs of the finished dishes—you've just been looking at in glossy magazines and expensive cookbooks. The glazed hams, the magnificent pheasants, the mounds of caviar . . . Then reality hits, and you begin to think about your pocketbook. The process starts over again. Maybe a roast, or some Veal Cordon Bleu . . .

Suddenly a voice inside you says, "How about an Eggplant Cordon Bleu instead? It'll taste every bit as good, and think of the money you'll save."

"It'll taste even better!" says a second inner voice. "And while you're at it, why not serve an entire vegetarian meal?"

Again reality takes hold. Sure, you've reached the point where you have enormous confidence in the ability of vegetable cookery to provide an infinite variety of wondrous tastes and textures. You've turned out dozens of successful dishes for your formerly skeptical family and you've even turned on some of your friends. But the fact is we're still pretty much a meat-oriented society, and many people are still victims of the days when *vegetarian* was synonymous with strange, bearded, turbaned, barefoot, chanting people, and vegetarian restaurants were inevitably small, less than immaculate, and patronized by hordes of the type described above.

Well, most of that has changed but the mythology lingers on, so I know where you're coming from if you're just a bit nervous

We are a meat-oriented society.

about something as radical as an all-veggie company dinner. Among the reasons I know where you're coming from: Recently I went onto Quube TV in Columbus, Ohio (a wondrous system that provides viewers with an opportunity to "talk back" to TV) and I asked the audience if they'd have the nerve to serve a vegetarian dinner to the Boss and his or her spouse. The results: 26 percent said yes, 74 percent no. And the yes vote was that high only because Columbus is the home of Ohio State University and lots of veggie-oriented students watch the show.

Anyway, as the self-appointed missionary of vegetarian cuisine, I say that there is no basis in reality for being afraid to serve a well-prepared, beautiful-to-look-at, delicious, filling vegetarian meal to anyone on this planet! People who love good food love any kind of good food, and people who don't love good food are nothing to worry about—they'll eat what they get and usually want seconds or thirds. (Remember the old joke: "The food in this place is terrible—and what's worse, they give such small portions!") Serving a vegetarian banquet has nothing to do with religion or ideology, it simply has to do with luscious, fresh, succulent dishes made of vegetables, nuts, cheese, and fruits.

In other words, when it comes to serving an all-vegetable meal, don't be chicken! Remember, rather than limiting the variety of food, an all-vegetable meal opens up almost infinite horizons that allow for several dishes of equal importance, as opposed to the traditional meat, chicken, or fish "main dish" menu. The table is an empty canvas upon which you are free to paint any meal that pleases the palette (that is, palate). There are some "rules,"to be sure, but, as in any art—writing, painting, composing—once you know the rules you're free to break them.

In the beginning, deciding on the menu will probably be far more difficult than the actual preparation of the dishes themselves. Ideally, of course, each menu should provide a balance: tart desserts to complement sweet side dishes; light salads with creamy soufflés; a variety of bright, fresh, vivid colors . . . all obvious things, to be sure, yet difficult for the average chef—let alone a relative novice—to put together. Perhaps the first thing to consider is your guests. Is there any particular food that any of them is allergic to or simply can't stand? Better safe

Once you know the rules you're free to break them.

than sorry. Call and find out if there's anything anybody *can't* eat. This done, let's think positive.

Which comes first, the chicken or the egg (or in our case, the chickpea or the eggplant)? Should you ponder first over the so-called "main course"? The answer is yes. There is one dish in every menu that can properly be identified as the centerpiece of the meal (unless it's an ethnic spread such as the Greek Platter), and it is around this dish that the rest of the meal will revolve. The nature of your "star" will definitely determine the makeup of the rest of the "cast."

Be mindful of what's in season (I've provided you with some lists) but better yet, take a trip to the market and see what looks especially good. Certain things will be lush, ripe, plentiful, and relatively inexpensive, while other things, if available at all, will either be second-rate or cost far too much. Not long ago, out of desperation, I bought two hydroponically grown tomatoes. Since tomatoes don't come into season here until mid- or late July, the tomatoes available during winter, spring, and late fall are your regulation pink Styrofoam jobs especially hybridized for maximum shipping durability. The hydroponically grown ones, however, are deep, rich red, firm yet gushing with thick, pulpy juice—in short, honest-to-God tomatoes. The problem? At $1.98 a pound I would be paying about $1.75 per tomato! (Oh, well, this February I did manage to resist the half pint of raspberries at $6.98.)

Next, start leafing through the menus and recipes to find ones that fit the produce you've decided to buy. Sooner or later you'll come upon a recipe that will be exactly right. Maybe it will be in this book, maybe in some other, perhaps in today's paper or a magazine that came last week.

However the choice is made, once you've settled on your main course you'll have to decide what you're going to surround it with. Do you want to begin with a salad? Or perhaps you'll feel like injecting a salad into the middle of the meal as a change of pace or to clear the palate, or maybe you'll put the salad near the end, right before dessert . . . or maybe you won't serve a salad at all. But if you do, what kind of lettuce should you use? Should it be plain lettuce, or lettuce with tomato, or perhaps a little avocado and some fruit on a bed of romaine. And what kind of dressing? There are so many choices. Roquefort, Vinaigrette, Sour Cream, Lemon-Mustard. . . . The good news is that practically any decision you make will be okay.

How about a soup along with the salad? Or instead of the salad? Often, on cold winter nights, Miss Page and I sit at our dinner table, overlooking our snow-covered garden, and make believe we're off in the country somewhere as we sup on a huge bowl of steaming Black Bean Soup, a crisp salad with vinaigrette dressing, and some crusty black bread or hot, homemade corn muffins. We have apples and cheese for dessert with homemade cappuccino.

Desserts. Of course you want dessert. I don't care what kind of diet you're on, allow yourself the joy of dessert at least once a week. (Miss Page and I recently joined the 1980s and went on a strict diet-and-exercise regime. Part of the reason we managed to do extraordinarily well and continue to this day is that once a week we indulge in what our friend Larry "Fats" Goldberg calls "Binge Day." We chose Sunday— and on that one day we can, and usually do, eat anything and everything that doesn't wiggle—pizza, omelets cooked in butter, hot fudge sundaes—and then we move on to lunch. . . .)

Oh—as Columbo used to say on TV—just one more thing. Lots of my recipes have little stories that just seem to go along. I hope you enjoy them as much as you do the recipes.

Bon appétit.

There's nothing quite so dull as a monochromatic meal.

Some Winter Menus

🥬 Vegetables, like any other sensible living creatures, are not thrilled about winter.

Thus, unless you live in a very temperate climate, most of your produce will have to be imported, which means extra cost and at least some loss of freshness and taste. And fruit lovers— those of us who truly *adore* fruit (*see* Fruit Salad)—find the winter months almost unbearable, let alone un-berry-able, in spite of the fact that apples are at their very best and the usual supply of citrus, pears, and melons is available.

Ah, but why belabor winter's negative side? Better to think of winter as a time for hot soups and steaming soufflés, fresh breads and mulled ciders. . . .

There are lots of good vegetables around during January, February, and March (which in this book will be defined as winter): avocados (which, if hard, must sit in the dark a couple of days to ripen), celery, cucumbers, endive, all kinds of lettuce, green peppers, beets, broccoli, Brussels sprouts, carrots, cauliflower, celery root, leeks, all manner of onions, all types of potatoes, and of course the super acorn, Hubbard, and butternut squashes. Come to think of it, there's really a fairly wide range available.

I think it would be fitting to start our winter menu section with a starter course: a brief discussion of soup.

Several soup recipes are included in these menus, and all call for water or vegetable bouillon. Making the bouillon is more trouble—peeling the walnuts, if you will—but in most cases definitely worth doing.

End of brief discussion.

A Winter Dinner Party

Here is a really elegant menu that includes a rich, creamy spinach soup. Remember, this soup, like many others, can stand alone as the centerpiece of a meal, accompanied only by a salad and warm, fresh bread, but as part of this menu, a small bowl is plenty.

🐚 *Beet Salad   Creamed Spinach Soup   Fresh Vegetable Crêpes   Grapefruit Ice*

Hail, Caesar! (Salad, That Is)

Legend has it that the Caesar salad was invented by a chef in a tiny restaurant in, of all places, Tijuana, Mexico. Whether that's true, or whether it was actually invented by Julius Caesar or Cesar Romero, I'm sure glad somebody invented it because even *without* the anchovies it's a dish fit for a king (or a queen).

🐚 *Caesar Salad   Mushroom Soup   Tangerine-Sweet Potato Bake   Apple Cake*

A Couple of Hours at Table

Last night I had a few friends over for dinner, and I spent about an hour in the kitchen, tossing together a very simple meal just using things that were lying about in the cupboards and fridge.

We sat down to eat, and I guess we were all starved because in less than ten minutes everybody was through! My friend Hal said, "What a shame! You spend all that time in the kitchen and poof—it's over like that!"

I nodded. It's true. Sometimes it's discouraging when you think of the hours you spend putting together a feast that's over and done in literally minutes. But isn't that what cooking is all about—enjoying the process of creating comestibles, and then reveling in the joy of watching your guests savoring every mouthful? What difference does it make how long they linger, as long as they love every bite and you've had a satisfying time preparing it?

Sometimes, however, a meal simply has to be eaten slowly. Each course is given its own solo presentation, followed by a few minutes of conversation before the next dish appears. The following menu begs for this "star treatment," if only because each individual dish is so absolutely satisfying and distinct. I suggest this menu for an especially cold night. Serve small portions, and eat the dessert around the fireplace, if you've got one.

Salad with Roquefort Sour-Cream Dressing   Split Pea Soup   Russian Vegetable Pie   Pears with Ginger

Fettuccine Alfredo

The more adventurous I become in the kitchen, the less inclined I am to eat out. I don't mean that to sound arrogant. It's just that it's getting harder and harder for me to reconcile paying the current and rising restaurant prices for things that I know I can make just as well myself for less than half the price. Certainly, I like to eat out from time to time, but unless it's a gala event, the dining-out experience is really just an excuse to have somebody else do the cooking and cleaning up, a luxury becoming ever more difficult to afford.

Fettuccine Alfredo is the latest dish I've decided I can do just as well at home as any restaurant can (Where I've paid as much as $9.50 for the pleasure). Don't ask me why, but for years I considered that particular cheese-and-pasta wonder to be something that required a magic touch to prepare. I was convinced you had to have an Italian accent to do justice to this most delectable of pastas.

Well, I was wrong. The accent doesn't matter a bit. If you follow my recipe it's guaranteed fail-safe. It is also, as you will quickly note, definitely in contention for the world's-most-fattening-recipe award. Try to remember that if you were eating out it would cost you nearly ten dollars a portion, so only make it if you feel you really can afford to splurge.

🍂 *Escarole with Lemon-Mustard Dressing*   *Fettuccine Alfredo*   *Braised Parsnips*   *Cherries Jubilee*

A Fantasy Come True

& For years I've had this wondrous fantasy, and not long ago
it came true. I'm going to tell you about it, but no need to send
the children out of the room because it's only about a cappuccino machine. Most precisely put, for years I fantasized about
owning a cappuccino machine and being able to make my own
cappuccino; at last, I do and I can!

In the beginning the fantasy involved owning one of those
great big copper-and-gold professional machines, but I knew
that this was impractical and beyond my financial reach—past,
present, or future. So for one of the very few times in my life
I lowered my sights and started casting about for a good,
serviceable machine that would realistically fit into both my
kitchen and my budget. It turned out that the kind I had in
mind—a much smaller but still copper-and-gold version of the
big one—would cost in the neighborhood of $300, a neighbor-
hood still too rich for me.

I guessed I'd have to wait until a windfall came—a big re-
sidual check or maybe a tax refund—and then one day I saw a
sign in the window of my neighborhood coffee and tea em-
porium: CAPPUCCINO MACHINE—SPECIAL SALE—$95."

I stopped and looked at the little machine in the window. It
was small—very small, about the size of an eight-cup percola-
tor—and completely undistinguished. To the machines I'd
been dreaming of it was like a peahen to a peacock. Stainless
steel with a steam pipe and an espresso dripper—in a word,
Unglamorous.

I went inside. The proprietor, Hugh, is a friend of mine, and I
knew he wouldn't steer a regular customer wrong.

"Tell me the truth, Hugh," I said. "Is that little cappuccino
machine really any good?"

"Of course it's good!" he said, just a mite indignant. "It makes espresso and cappuccino that taste just as good as any that come from those thousand-dollar machines."

"Then how come it's so cheap?" I asked, still skeptical.

He sighed. "Because it's stainless steel instead of copper, because you have to put it over heat instead of plugging it in, and because it's all you need if you want to make eight delicious cups of espresso! Would I steer you—a regular customer—wrong?"

My cash was on the counter before he'd finished his spiel.

"Sold," I said, and eagerly rushed home with my little machine and a pound of espresso beans.

Well, it took me a few tries to get it down perfectly, but as of last night, Miss Page and I agree that this little machine is one of the best investments we've ever made. We can have cappuccino any time we want it—including for breakfast, which is one of life's five great luxuries. We can really impress our friends at the end of a dinner party, and at an average restaurant cost of $1.50 a cup, we've already paid for it and then some.

The moral of this little tale? Maybe it's "Be it ever so humble, there's nothing like homemade." Or maybe it's "Sometimes big and flashy isn't really necessary to provide good results." (Is that too on-the-nose, do you think?) Anyway, there's definitely a moral in there someplace, so I think I'll ponder the question over a cup of hot, foamy homemade cappuccino. Liberally sprinkled with cinnamon, of course.

A Winter Warmer

Here is a winter menu that's delicious and filling and just perfect for a cold, snowy night. I know, because Miss Page and I just finished eating it, and I was almost too full for dessert.

🐦 *Apple and Celery Soup   Salad with Green Goddess Dressing   Sweet Shepherd's Pie   Lemon Roll*

I was just looking over my original notes for this book, made months ago, and noticed I'd planned to include a menu or two specifically for children.

What could I have been thinking of? Why should children have to eat in some special way different from that of adults? I guess I'd fallen victim to some mythology myself—that kids just automatically won't eat "good food," that they'll always opt for the junk if given the choice.

Nonsense! Hogwash! Kids are smarter than anybody; if a child is exposed to good, vegetarian cooking from the beginning and is painlessly instructed in the value of good nutrition as he or she creeps toward school age, odds are, when presented with choices offered by peers and "the outside world," the child will opt for that "really neat stuff" Mom or Dad cooks at home.

End of musing. Back into the kitchen.

Black Bean Soup Supper

There is only one thing surer than death or taxes: Offer to mail out free recipes on radio or TV and you'll be deluged with so many requests you'll wind up with gnarled, knotted, and neatly nicked hands from folding and stuffing envelopes, and a tired, tacky, twisted tongue from licking them closed.

In spite of my vow that each recipe I offer will be the last (frankly, there is no more boring and tiring job in the world than stuffing and licking envelopes), I find myself doing it again and again, simply because when I come across an extraordinary taste treat I feel obligated to share it with my listeners. (Besides, the voluminous mail always impresses the bosses!)

If I could single out one recipe for which I have received more requests than any other, it would be the one for Miss Page's Black Bean Soup. It was a cold, crisp winter afternoon when we gave that one out, and the response of SASE's (did you know that meant self-addressed stamped envelope? I only learned a week ago last Wednesday!) literally filled two entire mail sacks!

In fact, even though I offered that recipe over a year ago, requests still come in from time to time—the most gratifying (and irritating) being from people who'd gotten it before and then lost it.

Anyway, for all of you who've either lost it or never had it in the first place, you'll find the recipe on page 83 as the main event of a winter evening's hearty bill of fare.

🥢 *Bibb Lettuce with Vinaigrette Dressing*   *Black Bean Soup*   *Corn Bread*   *Chocolate Mousse*

It's Spring Again

"It's Spring again, the bird's on the wing again . . . my word, absurd—the wing is on the bird."

I'm sorry, but it seems as if I'm reminded of that song every spring, especially since I've moved back East where there actually are seasons! And spring is as nice a season as there is. Daffodils and tulips begin to poke their noses out of the ground, leaf buds begin to form on the trees—and tons of wonderful, fresh young vegetables begin to flood into the marketplace.

Asparagus prices come back to earth in the spring, as do California avocados and artichokes, chicory for salad, the first new lima beans, several spring varieties of potatoes, including the russet baker and new red and new white Florida boilers, and some spring varieties of squash: New Jersey acorn, butternut, and smaller versions of the summer squashes.

And now let me spring a little surprise: Did you know that cheeses have seasons? I am not a genuine expert on cheese, although I love it and can order, in the proper native dialect, St. André or Pipo Crème, Brie or Chèvre, or any number of other imported delicacies at my local cheeseteria, and I can heartily recommend cheese and fruit as a dessert any time of the year.

If you, as I, are fortunate enough to have a real *fromagerie* in your area, you'll be able to order a large selection of fine imported cheeses all year long. But in the spring, you'll find the Canadian sharp Cheddar especially good, and the Dutch Edam at its tangiest best, either making a perfect partner to any of the still crisp, juicy apples. A slice of soft American Liederkranz will go nicely with a bunch of California emperor grapes, and a wedge of Camembert will be the perfect complement to any of the many varieties of spring plums.

Most of the menus that follow are useful during any season of the year, but in April, May, and June they'll have a definite extra zing and when you step into the kitchen you'll have a little extra spring.

If You're Very, Very Hungary . . .

Here's a menu that has definite ethnic overtones; it seems designed for the 100 percent full-blooded glutton! But remember, small portions and tastes are the key to getting up from the table satisfied but not uncomfortable.

&❧ *Cucumber Salad with Paprika Dressing   Zucchini Loaf Hungarian Sour Potatoes   Chilled Apricot-Orange Crème*

Puttin' on the Ritz

Feel like really showing off? Here's a menu that sounds as ritzy as it tastes. (Do people still say "ritzy"?)

&❧ *Delmonico Salad   Garlic Soup   Vegetable Stroganoff   Rum Raisin Ice Cream with Flaming Rhubarb Sauce*

Eggplant Cordon Bleu

Remember earlier I spoke of Eggplant Cordon Bleu? Well here's a menu featuring this extremely tasty dish. I've included kasha in this particular menu because it's delicious as an occasional substitute for rice, bulgur, or millet. It's very pungent, however, so just add about two tablespoonfuls to each plate as an extraordinary "sponge" for the Creamy Tomato Sauce.

&❧ *Salad with Vinaigrette   Eggplant Cordon Bleu with Creamy Tomato Sauce   Kasha   Broccoli with Sauce Piquante   Hazelnut Cake*

Pasta Fazool!

I think I was about thirty before I knew that Pasta i Fagioli was the same thing as Pasta Fazool. (It is also the same thing as Pasta e Fagioli, but that comes out Pasta Fazool, too!)

Anyway, it was a few years after that that I learned how to make it, and it is only now that I pass along a recipe to you.

ᒪᕟ *Sweet and Sour Spinach Salad   Pasta i Fagioli   Brussels Sprouts with Garlic and Parmesan   Honeydew Melon Slices*

Open, Sesame!

You will note that one of the recipes in this menu calls for the use of sesame oil. You've probably seen it in lots of recipes. Sesame seeds have been used on casseroles, bread, and at funerals for forgiveness of sin. Maybe you've even used sesame oil in your own cooking; in case you haven't, you're in for a very special treat. Its peanutty taste is a great complement to sauces for vegetables, pastas, and salads. A word of warning: A little sesame oil goes a long, long way, so add the oil little by little, tasting as you go. Although sesame oil is expensive, it's worth it—so run, don't walk, to your nearest food store. Where might that be located? On Sesame Street, of course!

ᒪᕟ *Chicory with Vinaigrette   Sweet Potato Soup   Sesame Broccoli   Lima Bean Loaf   Chocolate Pie in Meringue Crust*

Binge Day

One of the things that has given us the courage, determination, and willpower to lose weight, in my case almost twenty pounds and in Miss Page's even more—we both now look (he said modestly) absolutely sensational, having begun a sensible, low-calorie, low-fat, 1,000 calorie-a-day diet and forty-five minutes of

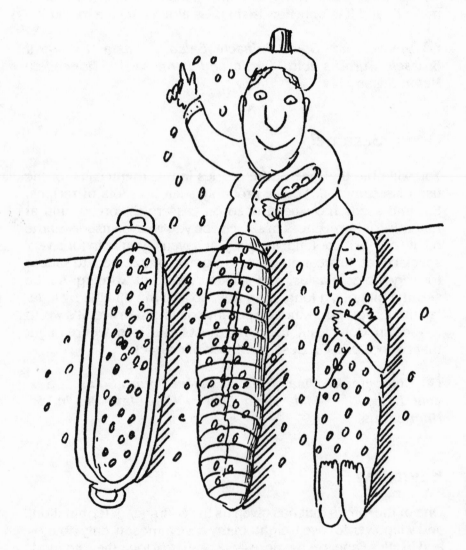

Sesame seeds have been used on casseroles, bread, and at funerals for forgiveness of sins.

daily exercise—has been the fact that on Sunday, affectionately known as Binge Day, we can eat anything we want. And usually do!

The concept of binging one or two days a week while conscientiously dieting the rest of the time was first presented to us, as I mentioned earlier, by Larry "Fats" Goldberg, who owns a pizzeria in New York (Goldberg's Pizza?) but who, over a period of several years, has managed to lose over 200 pounds and keep it off. In his excellent book, *Controlled Cheating*, Larry explains the theory in great detail. Suffice to say that starting a Sunday morning with three or four rich, buttery croissants or cheese Danishes, diving into a pizza with double extra cheese at lunch, and then cramming in a hot fudge sundae and half a Sacher torte after a six-course Mexican dinner will, indeed, show up as a pound or two on Monday morning. But by returning to the proper regimen at once—back to the bran cereal, fruit, and skim milk for that Monday morning breakfast—by Wednesday you'll notice you're beginning to lose weight again. And the best part is that on Friday, you can start thinking about what you're going to eat on Sunday, which not only gives you plenty of time to come up with a perfect Binge Day program, but makes the Spartan diet a lot more palatable while you wait.

One Sunday not long ago Miss Page and I decided to eat our Binge Day lunch at one of our favorite neighborhood restaurants, a vegetarian establishment. We knew before we set out what our dessert was going to be, as our friend Sally Stone had invited us over for her Ginger Cheesecake that's so rich and creamy it borders on the obscene. But the blackboard specials on Sunday afternoons are always a surprise treat, and this day was no exception.

The decision wasn't easy, confronted as we were with raging appetites and eight scrumptious-sounding entrées we'd never seen on the menu before. We finally made up our minds (after being reminded that seven couples had come and gone since we sat down and there *were* quite a few people waiting for a table) and settled on the following meal.

Since there's no waiting for a table here, won't you pull up a chair and join us for lunch and then a trip to Sally's for dessert.

🐦 *Vichyssoise   Mushroom Nut Salad   Vegetable Soufflé with Tahini   Sally's Ginger Cheesecake*

Cooking with Tofu (Or—Don't Throw Those Curds Away!)

I remember the time Miss Page came home and told me she was going to publish a book on cooking with tofu.

"I didn't know he was in town," I said.

"Don't be a wiseacre," she said, asking the impossible. "Tofu is going to be the next 'in' food, you'll see. It's going to become as popular as yogurt."

"Now just a minute," I said. "Yogurt is delicious, creamy, fruity. . . . Tofu is just bean curd any way you slice it. Or boil it, or sauté it . . ."

She shook her head. "Wrong, broccoli-breath! In case you've forgotten, when yogurt was first introduced it was available only in health food stores and was, to most people, just sour, bacteria-laden gunk that was like choking down medicine. It took a long time for people to accept yogurt as a wonderful, nourishing dessert or snack food."

"But tofu," I countered, "is just plain nothing! I mean, it's pure, unadulterated, tasteless texture!"

"Exactly!" She beamed triumphantly. "That's the whole key. It's got texture and it's tasteless, which means you can blend it with almost anything and it only costs pennies an ounce!"

"But"—I shook my head, puzzled—"if it's tasteless, why bother to mix it with anything, no matter how cheap it is?"

"Because," she said, "it's nature's number one source of protein, that's why! So by substituting tofu for cottage cheese, cream cheese, sour cream, mayonnaise, or yogurt, or just by adding it to other dishes to give them extra body . . . Here," she said, and handed me the book that had triggered this whole thing off.

It was a book called *Cook with Tofu* by Christina Clarke (Avon), and after I got through laughing at some of the recipes (Tofu Chocolate Mint Pie, in particular), I realized that not only are some of them really delicious, but it's quite true that there is absolutely nothing better as an additive and protein provider in many, many dishes. So here's a menu in which every dish includes soybean curd, or tofu. For you.

🍂 *Onion Soup   Salad with Creamy Herb Tofu Dressing
Baked Tofu Mozzarella   Chocolate Mint Pie*

FIDDLEHEADS

Have you ever seen or even heard of fiddleheads?

I'm not talking about people who are addicted to violin music; I'm talking about the early growth of the ostrich fern sold in some of the more exotic markets as fiddlehead greens.

The first time I encountered fiddlehead greens I was taken aback. Shocked, even. As Mr. Mother Earth, the very idea of eating a fern sounded like cannibalism! I mean, string beans and lettuce and snow peas and beets, they're living things in the plant kingdom, granted, but they, and most of their produce market brethren and sistren, are born to be eaten and dream of being taken home and delicately steamed or gently stir-fried. But a fern—that's another story!

Or is it?

I picked up one of those interesting fronds—shaped exactly as its name implies—and looked at it. Could this lovely piece of nature actually be food?

My research revealed that it is, indeed, not only food, but healthy and delicious food at that. The root of the fiddlehead, ostrich fern, grows in abundance along many North American rivers, being harvested mainly in New Brunswick and eastern Quebec. Fiddleheads are completely organic, as they grow wild, with no additives or artificial fertilizers.

It is only in early spring when the little fronds by Stradivarious poke their heads through the earth that the fiddleheads can be picked, for they very quickly uncurl and grow into tall, graceful ferns.

How do you eat a fiddlehead once you get over your initial distaste at the idea of eating a fern? You eat it boiled. (The fiddlehead is boiled, not you.) After you simmer it for ten or fifteen minutes until the fiddlehead is tender, you may want to serve it with a bit of butter, or a touch of pepper, or a vinaigrette salad dressing, or hollandaise. . . .

Anything that would taste good on a philodendron.

A Touch of Italy

Here's a fairly basic yet extremely varied and beautiful Italian presentation. Serve it to company on the next big Italian holiday—the Feast of San Gennaro, Columbus Day, or Joe DiMaggio's birthday. Whatever. *Buon Appetito!*

&❧ *Leeks with Caper Sauce   Minestrone   Cauliflower with Vinegar and Tomatoes   Granita di Limone*

A Greek Feast

Every now and then I get a longing for the Greek Islands. Ah, to sit beneath an olive tree, looking out over the Aegean . . . the Acropolis in the background, and a Mediterranean Greek platter in my lap!

Alas, I've never been to Greece, but I've been to lots of Greek restaurants (where I once did have a Greek platter spilled in my lap!). I often think there are more Greek restaurants in New York than in Athens—according to my friend Demitrius it's very, very close—but none is better than a tiny, home-style café near my apartment called Meandros.

Here's a typical Greek Binge-Day feast that I'm sure would have pleased the palate of even mighty Zeus himself.

&❧ *Greek Salad   Lemon Potatoes   Baba Ghanouj Hummus   Baklava*

For Very Special Occasions

This menu can be trotted out for *very* special occasions. Of course, as in any of the menus herein, the individual dishes can be prepared any time, any night, in any order.

&❧ *Avocado Salad with Crème Fraîche and Raspberry Vinegar Dressing   Cream of Leek, Potato, and Tomato Soup Spiced Cabbage   Mushrooms Polonaise   Lemon Soufflé*

A Greek feast.

Summertime!

❧ The best thing about summer in New York is the appearance of peaches and pears, melons and grapes and cherries—and best of all, berries at nearly affordable prices! Almost everything else that's available during the spring is available in summer, but obviously most meals will be lighter than those of other seasons: more salads, chilled soups, buffets, picnics.

What is generally unnecessary during the summer months is preparation of fancy desserts. Fresh fruits, eaten with crème fraîche or store-bought sorbet—or just enjoyed plain—will be the perfect ending to almost any meal. In this section, therefore, your choice of individual or mixed fruit will be the perfect finish for any menu instead of the suggested dessert.

A Star Is Born

One day I went to the market and the eggplants were the most beautiful I'd seen in years. Deep, rich purple, large, shiny, without blemishes—I couldn't resist buying a couple, figuring I'd make stuffed eggplant for dinner. Ah, but there was the rub. Stuffed with what? I looked around at the array of fresh, gorgeous produce surrounding me at the incredible Greenwich Village Italian market where we shop, then down into my shopping cart which contained a pound of freshly ground peanut butter, four cartons of yogurt, a head of Bibb lettuce, some scallions, and a bunch of celery.

There was a momentary pause as I surveyed the situation, and then the proverbial light bulb popped over my head. I finished my shopping by purchasing a large piece of fresh ginger-root, a huge, gloriously red pepper, an onion, and a pound of mocha-java beans. (For coffee, not the stuffed eggplant.)

When I got home I went right to work, and the result, Ginger Stuffed Eggplant, was a monumental success and has risen to genuine stardom since its auspicious debut.

🐝 *Iced Broccoli Cream Soup   Ginger-Stuffed Eggplant Green Beans with Basil   Spanish Lime Pie*

A Birthday Dinner

I don't know about you, but I look forward to my birthday. I look forward to Miss Page's birthday, too, although I'm not sure she's as enthusiastic as I.

Oh, I'm not into getting old, that's not it. It's just that we have a tradition, Miss Page and I: On my birthday she takes me to a big-time Broadway musical (the $50-a-ticket kind) and a very lavish, expensive dinner at some absolutely sensational restaurant where we'd never go unless it was a very special, special occasion; on her birthday, she gets the same treatment—Broadway musical and no-holds-barred feast.

Two absolute truths that have emerged during the past few years of this ritual are: 1) You can't go wrong not going to a Broadway musical and 2) The Coach House is one of the truly great restaurants in the world.

The menu below includes a basic bread custard from The Coach House that helps make any dinner just a bit more memorable.

🐝 *Mozzarella, Tomato, and Fresh Basil Salad   Asparagus Maltais   Summer Squash Soufflé   Bread Custard*

That Eggplant Roulade

This magnificent creation is a real showstopper. It can also be a real heart-stopper when it comes time to remove the roulade from the pan. Be sure you grease the bottom of the pan really well, and don't take it out of the oven until it's absolutely done. Topped with the Mornay sauce, this menu will have your friends suggesting you really ought to stop kidding around and open a vegetarian restaurant.

So why don't you?

🐁 *Tomatoes Stuffed with Cucumbers   Eggplant Roulade with Mornay Sauce   Celery Root Purée Frozen Peach Dessert*

In summertime, salads are often more than enough to be an entire meal.

That was the summer I discovered fruit salad.

August 1982

𝕖❧ That was the summer I discovered fruit salad.

No, of course I'm not talking about the cubed kind you get in little cans (heavy on the maraschino cherries) or even the kind I've been eating both at home and away most of my adult life—you know, lots of lovely fresh fruit, cut up and served with cottage cheese or sherbet.

I'm talking about the *ultimate* Fruit Salad, the only foodstuff that can truly claim the title "Ambrosia": that which caused me to look up at Miss Page one hot, steamy night and, while eating a spoonful, say, "You know, I think this is better than ice cream!"

Now if you knew our penchant for ice cream, you'd probably think that's an overstatement. And maybe you're right. But I swear, Fruit Salad à la Joel (yes, dammit, I'm going to take credit for this one!) is a magic carpet that will fly you directly to a semihypnotic state of epicurean bliss.

Why, only last night we had a couple of close friends over for dinner, and as I served each a heaping bowlful of my very best effort to date (it included several dozen fat, juicy black grapes I'd painstakingly halved and pitted), I was rewarded with a sigh from the end of the table. "Good God," said one of our guests, "I never realized that fruit salad could be this good. It's—it's like maybe the best thing I ever tasted!"

Our other guest nodded. "I think it's the juice. . . ."

I suppose there will be cynics who say, "Pooh. Fruit salad is fruit salad is fruit salad."

Well, cynics, I say to you perhaps you've just never prepared it right. You must turn the entire procedure into an adventure!

You start by very carefully picking the fruit. If you're lucky enough to own a fruit farm and can pluck your peaches or grapes or berries right from the trees or the vines or the

I owe it to Miss Page.

bushes, then you're in utopia. But even picking fruit at your local produce market can be a joy. Making sure the pineapple is of exactly the right color and ripeness; checking each plum, each nectarine, every apricot, the apples, bananas, cherries, grapes, pears, kiwis, strawberries, oranges, blueberries, mangoes, cantaloupes, casabas, cranshaws—every single kind of fruit that's available should be examined and the best three or four examples of each taken home.

Now get the biggest bowl you've got that'll fit in your fridge— save a whole shelf if you can; it's worth it—and start carefully cutting your fruit into bite-size pieces. Ideally, every piece of carefully cut fruit should be the same size. When you're through with all that—including pitting and tossing in the cherries—slice the pineapple in half, lengthwise. Now cut each half in half. Now carefully, with a sharp knife, remove the pineapple sections from the skin, remembering to squeeze the juice from the skin into your huge bowl of fruit. (Same with the melon rind. Usually, it'll be loaded with sweet, delicious juice.) Cut the pineapple into bite-size pieces and add it to the rest of the fruit.

Now add approximately one-half cup fresh orange juice, one-half cup grapefruit juice, and one-half cup pear juice.

Mix thoroughly with a wooden spoon and fork.

Add one pint frozen raspberry yogurt, mix again, cover the bowl tightly, and place it in the refrigerator to chill.

If, when you sit down to savor this celestial delight, you don't agree that fruit salad can definitely be in a class by itself— (Please fill in your own punch line. I have to run get a bowl.)

A Royal Artichoke

The first course of this menu—artichokes with blueberry rice— is actually traceable back to medieval times (although Ms. N'Og is not known to have tried it). The truth is, it's a dish fit for any night—or knight—and is as good today as it was in days of yore.

🐓 *Artichokes with Blueberry Rice*   *Vegetarian Casserole*
Sweet and Sour Carrots   *Indian Pudding*

The Borscht Circuit

My father and mother were in vaudeville, so I grew up hearing a lot about the "Borscht Circuit." Because my parents also liked to cook, borscht was a staple soup in our house, almost invariably served cold and garnished with grated beets and a huge dollop of sour cream. Over the years I've come to take my borscht straight, or with sour cream, or with chopped cucumbers, or even with all of the above.

This menu includes a Borscht that takes the sour cream just one extra step and includes buttermilk. It's these little extra steps that help get an act off the Borscht Circuit and onto the bill at the Palace. Or in this case, your house.

🍲 *Chilled Buttermilk Borscht   Green Bean Purée   Eggplant Newburg   Chocolate Sorbet*

Late-Summer Tomatoes

One of the great joys of late summer in New York is the opportunity to savor the rich, red, lush, juicy Jersey tomatoes which come to us in abundance from about the middle of July until the first or second week of September. Then, alas, it's back to those ridiculous pink, hard synthetics we discussed earlier.

The other day Miss Page was browsing through a food magazine. I was fanning myself with another to try and ward off the 90-degree weather (with 70 percent humidity) that only a Big Apple August can bring on.

"Here's an interesting recipe," she said and showed me a photograph of what appeared to be a very rich, red, cheese-topped tomato bake.

"It's a very rich, red, tomato bake," she said, and smiled almost gloatingly. How she reads my mind is a mystery, but the fact that she does is a given. "I think we ought to try it while we can still get good Jersey tomatoes."

The thought of a hot dish on this steamy day didn't exactly whack me between the eyes, but the dichotomy was there, all right. It was practically now or never.

"Let's wait until tomorrow," I said, hoping the weather might change.

And as if He were reading my mind, the next day rain poured and the temperature dropped down into the 60s! Honest!

Taking it as the Divine signal it was, I dashed out into the wintry day, picked up the necessary ingredients, and whipped up the Garden Tomato Bake. It tasted better than it looked in the photograph, and I'm convinced it would have been delicious even on the muggy, icky day before.

In fact it was, reheated, on the muggy, icky day after.

&❧ *Cuban Avocado Salad   Sautéed Fennel   Garden Tomato Bake   Pears and Ricotta*

I'll Be Right Back

There have been many times during the long months of compiling this book that I've jumped from the typewriter or the bookshelf or even gotten out of bed in the middle of the night to try a recipe I've just discovered that sounds out of this world.

Right now I simply have to take some time off and prepare this entire menu for company coming tonight. Please excuse me. I'll be right back.

&❧ *Tomato Ice   Bombay Rice-Stuffed Onions with Orange Glaze   Broccoli with Walnut Sauce   Blueberry Pudding*

The Conversion of Joey

It's always exciting to make a convert. I don't mean converting a meat-eater to a vegetarian, because as you know, I've got nothing against *your* eating meat. I chose to exclude meat from my diet some years ago because a meatless regimen seemed to me to be the most sensible, healthy way to eat. I remained on the diet long after most of my fad-following friends had deserted their salad days and eagerly surrendered to the Big Mac attack. I am still on it today (although I eat a piece of fish once in a while) because I'm more convinced than ever that red meat serves absolutely no useful purpose in your diet and, in fact, the evidence shows that there may even be

I eat a piece of fish once in a while.

some detrimental effects from animal fat. In addition, meat is terribly high in calories compared to any vegetable or fruit or even chicken and fish.

The kind of conversion I'm talking about is getting an unsophisticated eater to try something that is almost repugnant to him and then not only admit he likes it, but confess further that he loves it and could he please have just a teeny bit more?

Such was the case with my close friend Joey, a meat-and-potatoes man if there ever was one. Joey had always turned up his nose at my vegetarian offerings in the past—even though his favorite food, "a slice of Ray's pizza," is as vegetarian as it gets—but on this particular day, for whatever the reason, Joey said yes when I made the obligatory offer:

"I fixed some Eggplant Enchiladas last night. You want me to heat 'em up for lunch?"

Expecting the usual grimace and "No, thanks, I'm not hungry," I was shocked when he cocked his head and frowned, "Eggplant Enchiladas? Sure. Why not?"

Not wanting to press my luck, I didn't bother to ask why he'd suddenly decided to try one of my "weird, exotic dishes." I just turned on the oven, popped in the delectable-looking leftovers from our "fiesta" the night before, and prayed he wouldn't change his mind while they were heating.

He didn't. In fact, as the aroma began to float from the oven, his nose twitched and he smiled. "Smells good," he said.

"Wait till you taste them," I said. "I promise, you'll like them even better than meat or chicken enchiladas."

"That's for sure," he grinned. "I've never eaten those, either."

Well, I served up Joey's enchilada and held my breath while he took the first, tentative forkful. He grinned, then nodded. "You win," he said. "I love it."

Now, almost three years later, as Joey and I sat and chatted over our morning newspapers and coffee in the neighborhood restaurant where we meet a couple of days a week, Joey asked if I could give him the recipe so his wife, Barbara, could prepare them for their company dinner next week. I was honored to give it to him, and am equally honored to share it with you as the main course in this delicious Mexican menu.

❧ *Gazpacho*   *Eggplant Enchiladas*   *Rice with Beans and Cheese*   *Flan*

Fall

శ⤚ Fall, or autumn—all three weeks of it—is my favorite season. Just the right temperature, clear skies, the blessed relief between summer heat and winter cold. The changing leaves are beautiful, Halloween and Thanksgiving presage that most glorious of holiday seasons, Christmas (or Hanukah) and the coming New Year.

Gastronomically, there isn't a whole lot going on in the fall that isn't available at other times of the year—at least not for us vegetarians. (For the rest of you, however, fall is something of a bonanza, bringing with it the first batches of venison, ringneck pheasant, and succulent cuts of brown bear.) In fall your market will be filled with crisp, tasty produce, and the crisp, tasty weather will provide an ambience to complement all these foods.

A few basic tips about fall cookery: Almost all your salad greens will be a little sharp now, so use a stronger blend of aromatic herbs and spices in making vinaigrette dressing; with the harder cold-weather vegetables follow the same advice: more dominant flavorings and sauces than you'd use in spring or summer. And, of course, it's the season for lots of pudding-type desserts.

Turkeyless Thanksgiving

One of the great joys of being a vegetarian is not having to eat turkey at Thanksgiving. Actually, I suppose turkey isn't all *that* bad—even though it's synomonous with *flop* and nobody eats turkey at any other time of year—but if you think about it, around 90 percent of the traditional Thanksgiving feast is vegetarian anyway, so even without the turkey it's a bonanza for vegetarians.

The other morning, as my bright, energetic, and indispensable assistant/researcher, Allyson, pondered the menu for her upcoming Thanksgiving gathering, she looked up from her list of seasonal vegetables and asked, "How do you feel about beets?"

"Beets?" I exclaimed. "Why, everybody knows how I feel about beets. I'm a regular beet-and-potatoes man. I'm a member of the Beet Generation. You just can't beat a good beet. . . ."

"I know, I know." She groaned. "I read your last cookbook. You did this whole number on beets—they can be sliced into strips cooked or raw and can be made into borscht and blah blah blah— But you didn't really have a recipe for a main dish starring beets."

I frowned. She was right. And right off the top of my head I couldn't think of ever having eaten one or even read a recipe for one anywhere.

"The time has come," I said with fierce determination, "to think up a main dish for beets!"

That night I told Miss Page I'd had a great idea: "A main dish where beets are the main ingredient!" I cried triumphantly.

"So?" She waited. "What is it?"

I shrugged sheepishly. "Well, I can't think of *everything*. . . ."

A few minutes later we'd arrived at a raw, basic idea: Why not take the general ingredients of a beet borscht and go from there into another format?

The next day I rushed off to the market, the beginnings of the recipe's structure in my mind. I knew I wanted beets—and I'd decided to include potatoes and onions—and then, suddenly, I saw the fresh cranberries, and—*Voilà!* Eureka! Well I'll be damned! I had an idea for a beet main dish that would surely be a showstopper.

That night I presented Miss Page with a first draft of my creation. I'd used the beets, onions, cranberries, and other good stuff but I'd switched over to sweet potatoes for the sake of an autumnal color display.

She tasted, she nodded, she tasted again, then said, "It's delicious. It's superb. But if I were you, I'd bake it in a pie and add a layer of tofu."

I am a member of the "Beet Generation."

As usual, her creative and thoughtful touch was just what was needed. And so, here publicly unveiled for the first time, is the Mother Earth Thanksgiving Feast, starring Beets and Sweets and featuring an array of dazzling supporting players. This is one Thanksgiving feast I can promise isn't a turkey!

𝄞 *Cucumber and Cheese Salad   Corn Fritters with Cran-apple Relish   Creamed Onions   Beets and Sweet Potato Pie   Pumpkin Pudding*

Curried Carrot Soup

This menu features one of the most delicate soups I've ever run across. And if there's still room at the end of the meal, you'll absolutely swoon over dessert.

𝄞 *Curried Carrot Soup   Lemon Asparagus   Cold Eggplant Provençale   Vanilla Ice Cream with Peanut Butter Sauce*

The Cardinal Sin of Cooking

What's the worst mistake a cook can make?

Seems there are so many it'd be hard to choose one, but I have. It took a lot of thought, but I finally eliminated overcooking (forgetting to set the timer), burning, using too much spice (once added, a pinch-turned-tablespoon can be, and usually is, fatal to any dish)—you name it.

The cardinal sin of cooking is forgetting to put on an apron.

Witness the $8.50 cleaning bill I just paid because I committed this sin last Saturday night while I was putting together the menu below. Oh, it shouldn't be a total loss. By sharing the menu with you in this book, maybe I can deduct the cleaning bill from my taxes!

𝄞 *Mushrooms with Eggplant and Tomato   Corn Soufflé   Peas with Cream and Mint   Sticky Gingerbread*

Millet? Let's Mull It

Not too many people are familiar with millet, which is too bad because millet is a terrific substitute for rice, bulgur, oatmeal, or even a hot fudge sundae if you're kinky enough.

Millet is a member of the Grass family (you know his brothers Crab and Dichondra) that is cultivated mostly in Africa and sold almost exclusively in health food stores. This recipe is a good one and something you should have in your collection to do with as you see fit—but preferably eat, because a millet lawn can be a trial to keep up.

3 tablespoons oil
1 onion, chopped fine
½ teaspoon dried oregano
2 cups water
1 cup millet

Heat oil in frying pan, then sauté onion until tender. Add oregano, then sauté another five minutes.

About 1 hour before serving, heat water to boiling in a saucepan, add millet, cover, and cook over low heat for about 20 minutes. Adjust the heat as you would for rice. After 20 minutes, remove from heat and allow to stand, covered, for 30 minutes. Warm the onion mixture and just before serving, add to the millet mixture and stir well.

Serves 6.

A Marriage Made in Heaven?

❧ One of the fun things about reading restaurant reviews is the wonderful language a good food writer uses when describing subtleness of tastes and textures. ("The tomato consommé displayed a hint of basil, and the superb date-nut torte was lightly dusted with powdered sugar and cinnamon.")

And then there's my favorite, the classic, oft-repeated references to how well certain foods or spices "marry" with one another. ("The ginger sauce and the limes made a perfect marriage.")

Well, recently I ordered a bowl of creamed corn chowder at one of my favorite local restaurants and was a little startled, when it came, to discover that the chef had really gone heavy on the garlic. I happen to like garlic, and there certainly wasn't too much garlic—it just seemed a bit odd . . . corn and garlic . . . it hadn't occurred to me before. I've always preferred my corn just boiled for an instant or roasted in the husk, then slathered with butter and pepper, but it was a good marriage, this one between corn and garlic, so I decided to pass the recipe along to you. You can plan the nuptials for any time, since corn is in peak season now, and you'll be grateful to know that this wedding is going to cost practically nothing.

Before I let you go, however, I thought you might be interested to know how the original announcement appeared in the *New York Times*:

Carol "Sweet" Corn, daughter of Kernel Corn and Mrs. Wilhelmina Maize of Strong Sun Garden, Iowa, was married yesterday to Gary Garlic, son of Sam Shallot and the late Mrs. Olivia Onion. The ceremony was performed by Chef Pierre Potage in the kitchen of Veggies, Inc. The former Miss Corn graduated with flying tassels from Elephant's

67

Eye High School and Cob College, and Mr. Garlic is self-employed scaring off vampires.

Okay, it was corny. So sue me. But I think you'll forgive me after you savor the soup as part of this a-maizingly good menu. (Ouch, okay, I'm sorry. . . .)

🐛 *Beet and Endive Salad*   *Corn-Garlic Chowder*   *Vegetables with Ginger*   *Ice-Cold Honeydew Melon Slices*

Not Exactly Huevos Rancheros

About five times during the past two weeks, my assistant, Allyson, has brought up the subject of Huevos Rancheros. On each occasion, I've said no to including the recipe on the grounds that A) although I personally love Huevos Rancheros as a breakfast dish when I'm in Southern California, this book is essentially about gourmet vegetarian dinners, and B) I used that recipe in my last book.

Today she brought it up again with a renewed plea: "A, where's the law that says if something is good for breakfast it won't be just as good for dinner? Most nutritionists agree we'd all be better off eating our heavy meal in the morning and light meal at night. And B, I've come up with a terrific, brand-new variation. Not your usual Huevos Rancheros."

So I looked, I tried, I cried "*Olé,*" and I gave in.

🐛 *Stuffed Avocado*   *Huevos Rancheros*   *Pepper-Corn Bake*   *Cocada*

Artichoke-Stuffed Artichoke
I feel like Ms. N'Og.

I think I just invented a recipe, in spite of my previous protestation that there is no such thing as a new recipe. But there's a saying that the exception proves the rule, and artichoke stuffed with artichoke might just be it.

What happened was, I had this artichoke lying there in the

Not exactly Huevos Rancheros.

refrigerator, and I knew that if I didn't eat it tonight I'd have to throw it away, and I hate throwing out dead food almost as much as I hate throwing out dead plants. So I decided to steam the artichoke and then eat it, stuffed, until I was stuffed, but unfortunately I didn't have any stuff to stuff it with and it was too late to go to the market. . . .

So I stuffed it with itself.

Okay, I'm sure that by now you've dug up nine recipes that use artichoke heart as the basis for the stuffing of an artichoke. I doubt if any are as satisfying as this invention, mothered by necessity.

🖝 *Artichoke-Stuffed Artichoke*　　　*Mushroom Stew*
Glazed Squash　　*Raspberry Whip*

Visitors to the East

🐌 Miss Page and I recently went on a tour of the Far East. I mean the real Far East as opposed to the Hamptons, and I mean a real tour, as opposed to a rambling holiday. We went to seven places in twenty-one days—Tokyo, Kyoto, Hong Kong, Bangkok, Singapore, Jakarta, and Bali—and traveling with a group of twenty-four other hardy souls, we flew close to 30,000 miles.

Boy, are my arms tired!

But seriously . . .

This trip was the culmination of a lifelong dream. I've always longed for a close personal look at the mysterious East—having grown up as a film buff during the forties who particularly savored movies in which spies and traitors scuttled about the Long Bar in Singapore or the back alleys of Hong Kong while Sydney Greenstreet held forth with lines like "This is Macau, my friend. Sooner or later, everyone must come to Macau!"

Well, I've been to Macau.

It wasn't easy deciding where to go. We confronted the tour brochures and the maps much as one might grapple with the menu at a particularly wonderful restaurant. Good God, it all looks so delicious. And we'll probably never get here again . . . oh, if only I could have just a little taste of everything . . . like a buffet. . . .

Okay, we decided, that's what we'd do. We'd have a taste of Tokyo, a cup of Kyoto, a spoonful of Singapore, a bite of Bali, and Hong Kong for dessert.

Like a great buffet upon which each dish has been lovingly prepared by a master chef—such was our trip. I would like to be able to recreate it for you because those three weeks were probably the most intensely ingratiating of my life. Another

71

Visitors to the East.

world, indeed! A mind-boggling kaleidoscope of cultures: How can Tokyo, with a population of 11 million and looking very much like New York, manage to be so clean you could eat off the floor of the subway? How could poverty-stricken children along the banks of a river in Bangkok all have such huge, friendly smiles as they waved at us cruising by in a sight-seeing boat? And how could the most magnificent palace on the planet not only sit majestically in the midst of such poverty, but even be revered by the very poorest Thai?

Only now, a couple of weeks since returning, have I begun to see bits and pieces of the trip as actual, full-blown incidents (the development of my forty rolls of film didn't hurt this process, I'm sure). I remember the Floridian in Singapore who declined to tour the Botanic Garden because "we got the same kind of foliage where I come from." (I thought that would be like not going into the Louvre because they use the same kind of paint where I come from. . . .) And then that same man, that same night, proudly announced he'd just had the best dinner he'd had yet on the trip. He'd found a Kentucky Fried Chicken stand!

Anyhow, that part of the trip is for another time. Right now my memories focus on food. When we decided to take the trip in the first place, we began to think about the infinite wonderments of vegetarian cookery that surely would unfurl in this, the center of vegetarian cuisine. We discovered right away, however, that for the vegetarian tourist there are some pitfalls in Paradise. In Japan, for instance, it's impossible to find simple steamed vegetables! Sukiyaki? All you can eat. Tempura? Every third restaurant. Sushi, pizza, hamburgers, Chinese food —endless. And yet perhaps our most memorable dining experience of the trip took place in Kyoto, at a restaurant called Hyotei (expensive, like The Palace in New York or Maxim's in Paris, but worth every yen).

In Bangkok our best meal was in the Castillon Dining Room of the Dusit Thani Hotel, although we did enjoy an excellent repast at the Indra Grill.

The Chinese food in Hong Kong was superb, especially at the Man Wah Restaurant in the Mandarin Hotel and at the world-famous Red Chili Szechwan Restaurant.

The highlight in Singapore was a visit to the fabled Long Bar in the Raffles Hotel; however, the food in the equally fabled Elizabethan Room was virtually inedible. A small local restaurant, the Rendezvous, turned out to be the culinary high point of that absolutely scintillating and most exciting city.

The food in Bali was okay, but one doesn't really go there for food so I can't say anything there was truly memorable except for the superb Gado-Gado.

Another time, another place, another book—that's when I'll describe the myriad wonders of this most unforgettable trip. But for the time being, here is a menu that represents the types of food you should not only expect but savor if you ever get the opportunity to go to this most mystical part of the world.

✺ *Mee Siam (Singapore)   Gado-Gado (Bali)   Rice with Chiles, Tomatoes, and Coconut (Bangkok)   Szechwan Eggplant (Hong Kong)   Glazed Banana (Hong Kong)   Mangoes and Sticky Rice (Bangkok)*

Appetizers

Artichoke-Stuffed Artichoke

6 large artichokes
1 cup mayonnaise
Juice of 2 lemons

Trim artichokes, cutting off bottoms and spines. Place artichokes in large saucepan with about 4 inches of water, cover, and cook over medium heat for 30–40 minutes or until artichokes are tender. Remove artichokes from pan, and carefully open each until leaves are spread almost flat and thistle-covered heart is exposed. Carefully cut "heart" from center of each artichoke, and cut and scrape away all thistle from top. Cut artichoke hearts into small chunks. Mix mayonnaise and lemon juice in a bowl. Stir in artichoke heart pieces, mashing them slightly to create a lumpy paste. Stuff each artichoke with this mixture, which is also excellent as a dip for tender ends of artichoke leaves.

Serves 6.

Baba Ghanouj

6 large eggplants
Juice of 2 lemons
2 tablespoons tahini or sesame paste
Salt

1 large clove garlic
¼ cup chopped parsley or pomegranate seeds
2 tablespoons olive oil

Cook whole, unpeeled eggplants over charcoal or over a slow-to-medium gas flame. Cook eggplants on all sides, turning as necessary, until they are soft throughout and skin is charred. Set aside for about 1 hour to cool.

Peel eggplants and discard skin. Put flesh into a mixing bowl and immediately add lemon juice. Mash well. Add tahini and blend well. Add salt to taste.

Place garlic clove between sheets of waxed paper and mash and pound gently with a mallet or the bottom of a skillet. The garlic should be mashed as fine as possible. Add mashed garlic to eggplant mixture, stir well, and chill. Place in a flat serving dish and garnish with parsley or pomegranate seeds. Pour olive oil over the dish and serve as an appetizer.

Serves 8.

Eggplant Roulade

1¼ pounds zucchini
Salt
1 medium eggplant (about 1 pound)
2 tablespoons olive oil
2 cups peeled, cooked tomatoes, with liquid
2 teaspoons sugar
2 teaspoons lemon juice
⅓ cup cream
Pepper
½ cup butter
⅓ cup chopped onion
⅔ cup flour
1 cup warm milk
4 eggs, separated
½ cup grated Parmesan cheese

Fine, dry bread crumbs
½ cup pine nuts
Mornay Sauce (recipe on page 161)

Wash and grate zucchini, and toss with 1 teaspoon salt. Place zucchini in a colander to drain for 20 minutes. Then squeeze out excess moisture from grated zucchini, rinsing first only if too salty.

Peel and grate eggplant. Sauté grated eggplant for 10 –15 minutes in olive oil, stirring often. Add tomatoes, sugar, and lemon juice, and cook over medium-high heat, stirring almost constantly until sauce is thick. Add cream, salt, and pepper, and continue cooking until mixture is no longer runny.

Preheat oven to 375°.

Melt butter in a medium saucepan, and sauté onion until it is completely transparent. Stir in flour and continue stirring, over low heat, until flour is golden, about 5 or 6 minutes. Add warm milk and stir vigorously until mixture is smooth and thick. Remove pan from heat and allow to cool for 5 minutes. Beat in egg yolks, then stir in zucchini and Parmesan cheese.

Beat 4 egg whites until fairly stiff. Stir half the egg whites thoroughly into egg-zucchini-cheese mixture, then fold in the other half.

Butter a 10″ × 14″ jelly roll pan and sprinkle with bread crumbs. Spread zucchini mixture evenly over the entire surface of the pan. Bake for about 15 minutes, or until mixture is puffed and coming away from the sides.

Turn roulade out on a tea towel. Spread eggplant filling onto roulade, leaving a 1½-inch border along one side. Sprinkle pine nuts over filling and, starting with the end where the border has been left, roll it up lengthwise. Use towel to help roll evenly.

Put roulade back in oven for 5 minutes. Serve with Mornay Sauce.

Serves 6 to 8.

Hummus

1½ cups cooked chickpeas
⅓ cup sesame oil
½ cup fresh lemon juice
1 garlic clove, mashed
Salt
Freshly ground pepper
Lettuce
2 tablespoons minced parsley or chopped fresh mint

Press chickpeas through a sieve or a food mill. Stir in sesame oil and lemon juice. Stir in garlic and season lightly with salt and pepper. There should be a smooth purée with the consistency of sour cream. If too thick, beat in a little water, 1 tablespoon at a time. Pile on a plate lined with lettuce and sprinkle with parsley or mint. Chill before serving.

Serves 4 to 6.

Note: This can be made in a blender, though the texture will be rougher because the chickpea skins are blended in. To assemble, blend together sesame oil, lemon juice, and garlic. Add chickpeas. Cover and blend at high speed. If too thick, add a little water, 1 tablespoon at a time. Then proceed as above.

Fresh Mushrooms with Eggplant and Tomato

1 1-pound eggplant
Sea salt or coarse salt
3 tablespoons olive oil (preferably cold-pressed)
1 medium yellow onion, finely chopped
1 large celery stalk, finely chopped
2 medium, firm mushrooms, coarsely chopped
1½ teaspoons finely chopped garlic
1 large or 2 medium ripe tomatoes, peeled and coarsely
  chopped
2 tablespoons dry whole-wheat bread crumbs

Leave your friends as stuffed as the mushrooms.

1 tablespoon tomato paste
5 tablespoons finely chopped fresh parsley
1 teaspoon dried basil
Fresh lemon juice
30 medium, firm whole mushrooms

Cut eggplant in half lengthwise. Make crisscross pattern in pulp and sprinkle with salt. Let stand 30 minutes.

Rinse eggplant thoroughly and drain well; pat dry with paper towels. Peel eggplant, and coarsely chop pulp.

Heat 2 tablespoons oil in medium skillet over medium-low heat. Add eggplant and cook until softened, about 2 minutes. Remove from pan and let cool.

Heat remaining oil in same skillet over medium heat. Add onion, celery, chopped mushrooms, and garlic, and cook 3–4 minutes. Return eggplant to skillet with tomatoes. Stir in bread crumbs, tomato paste, and 3 tablespoons parsley. Add basil, and continue cooking over medium heat about 4 minutes. (Mixture can be prepared ahead to this point, covered, and refrigerated.)

Just before serving, dampen paper towel with mixture of water and small amount of lemon juice. Wipe whole mushrooms lightly. Carefully remove stems. Fill each cap with some of stuffing. Sprinkle with remaining parsley, and serve.

Mushrooms can also be served hot. Run under broiler or bake briefly to warm through before sprinkling with parsley.

Makes 30 hors d'oeuvres. (Serves 6.)

Tomato Ice Appetizer

8 large tomatoes, peeled, seeded, and chopped
¾ cup chopped onion
¾ cup chopped celery
2 tablespoons sugar

2 tablespoons fresh lemon juice
1 teaspoon Worcestershire sauce
6 sprigs fresh mint or 2 teaspoons dried, crumbled mint
2–3 drops Tabasco (hot pepper sauce)
2 small garlic cloves, crushed
Mint sprigs

Combine all ingredients except mint sprigs in food processor or blender and purée until smooth. Taste and adjust seasoning. Mixture should be highly seasoned as freezing tends to diminish flavor. Pour into shallow container and freeze.

Spoon frozen mixture into processor or blender and mix until fluffy (or transfer to medium bowl and beat with electric mixer). Return to shallow container, cover, and freeze until firm. Just before serving, divide among 6 wineglasses and garnish with mint sprigs.

Serves 6.

Soups

Apple and Celery Soup

3 tablespoons vegetable oil
2 large celery stalks, sliced
1 medium yellow onion, sliced
1 medium carrot, sliced
5 medium apples, unpeeled, cored and thinly sliced
1 cup water mixed with 2 teaspoons tamari soy sauce
1 cup apple juice
1 cup milk
Yogurt

In vegetable oil, sauté celery, onion, and carrot for 4–5 minutes in 4-quart saucepan. Add apples; increase heat to high and cook, stirring occasionally, until apples are soft, about 5–10 minutes. Add water, juice, and milk and bring to a boil. Reduce heat and simmer about 5–10 minutes. Transfer mixture in batches to blender, and purée. Return purée to saucepan, adding more milk if it is too thick. Heat soup through over low heat.

Ladle soup into bowls. Garnish each with about 1 tablespoon yogurt. Serve hot or chilled.

Serves 6.

Black Bean Soup

1 pound black beans (check label to see if they must be
   soaked before cooking)
8 cups water
2 tablespoons salt

1 cup finely chopped onion
1 cup finely chopped green pepper
1 cup finely chopped celery
1 cup finely chopped carrots
8 tablespoons olive oil
6 garlic cloves, chopped
1 tablespoon ground cuminseed
4 teaspoons white vinegar
1 teaspoon soy sauce

Simmer beans in salted water until soft.

Sauté onion, green pepper, celery, and carrots in olive oil until onions turn golden brown. Add garlic, cumin, vinegar, and soy sauce. Cook, stirring, for about 3 minutes.

Drain about ½ cup water from beans, and add it to sautéed vegetables. Cook this mixture over a low flame for about 30 minutes.

Combine vegetables with beans. Add more water if necessary. Cook for another 30 minutes.

Serve garnished with any of the following: sieved hard-boiled egg yolks, chopped raw onion, a dollop of sour cream, or grated cheese.

Serves 6 as main course.

Chilled Buttermilk Borscht

5 large fresh beets
4 cups water
1 teaspoon salt
1 medium cucumber
½ cup very finely minced scallions
6 teaspoons honey
Fresh black pepper

1 tablespoon fresh chopped dill (or ½ teaspoon dried
  dillweed)
2 cups buttermilk
Sour cream

Peel and quarter beets. Place beets in saucepan with water and salt, and cook, covered, for 15 minutes over medium heat. Let beets stand until cool enough to handle. Remove beets with a slotted spoon, coarsely grate them, and return them to cooking water. Add all remaining ingredients, except buttermilk. Mix well. Chill.

Whisk in buttermilk before serving. Garnish with a spoonful of sour cream.

Serves 6.

Iced Broccoli Cream Soup

4 cups Vegetable Bouillon (recipe on page 95)
1 pound broccoli
2 medium yellow onions, chopped
3 small carrots, scraped and sliced
1 white celery heart, chopped
Fresh parsley
Cayenne pepper
1½ tablespoons ground arrowroot
1 cup half-and-half
Rosemary
1 bunch green scallions

Heat vegetable bouillon in a large saucepan. Cut flowerets from broccoli and set aside. Cut up stalks into chunks, and drop them into simmering bouillon. Add chopped onions, carrots, chopped celery heart, a small handful of parsley, chopped, and cayenne pepper to taste. Simmer, covered, for 15 minutes. Put broccoli flowerets into a small saucepan, and add enough hot liquid from larger pot to cover broccoli. Simmer flowerets for 5 minutes, strain liquid back into main pan, and chill flowerets for later garnish. Put 3 teaspoons arrowroot into a cup and liquefy with 1–2 tablespoons of half-and-half. Turn off heat under large pan, and blend in arrowroot mixture, stirring vigorously until liquid is thickened to consistency of light cream. Stir in a bit more arrowroot if necessary to thicken. Purée in blender, then pour in a covered dish, stir in about ½ teaspoon dried rosemary, and chill for several hours.

Just before serving, remove from refrigerator and blend in remaining half-and-half. Serve in chilled bowls. Garnish each serving with broccoli flowerets and finely chopped scallion tops.

Serves 6.

Curried Carrot Soup

1 onion, chopped
2 tablespoons olive oil
1 pound carrots, chopped (about 4 cups)
2 cloves garlic, minced
½ teaspoon mustard seed
½ teaspoon turmeric
½ teaspoon ginger
½ teaspoon cumin
¼ teaspoon cinnamon
⅛ teaspoon cayenne
1 tablespoon lemon juice
1 cup water
3 tablespoons butter
3 tablespoons flour
4 cups milk
1 tablespoon honey
Yogurt

Sauté onion in olive oil until golden. Add carrots, garlic, spices, and lemon juice. Cook 2–3 minutes, stirring constantly. Add water, cover pan tightly, and simmer until carrots are tender, about 20 minutes.

Purée mixture in a blender or sieve, adding small amounts of milk, if necessary. Be careful to fill blender no more than half full; start it on low speed, and hold top on tightly.

In a saucepan, melt butter and add flour. Cook for 2–3 minutes, stirring often. Add milk and honey, stirring constantly with a whisk. Cook sauce over medium heat, stirring fairly constantly, until sauce is very hot.

Combine sauce with carrot purée, and heat until very hot, about 10 minutes. Serve hot with a spoonful of yogurt on top.

Serves 8.

Corn-Garlic Chowder

2 cups fresh corn kernels (from 5 or 6 ears of corn)
3 cups Vegetable Bouillon (recipe on page 95) or water
½ teaspoon sugar
½ cup minced onion
¼ cup minced celery
¼ cup butter
½ teaspoon dry mustard
Pepper
1 tablespoon lemon juice
4 garlic cloves, chopped fine
2 cups milk
Dash Tabasco (hot pepper sauce)
1 egg yolk, beaten
1 cup heavy cream
1 teaspoon salt
Paprika
Parsley

Scrape kernels from corn, then boil cobs in bouillon or water with sugar for 15 minutes. Strain and reserve stock.

Sauté corn kernels, onion, and celery in butter with mustard and pepper until onion is transparent. Add lemon juice, reserved stock, and garlic; cover, bring to boil, and simmer for 10 minutes. Add milk and Tabasco, then beat egg yolk and heavy cream, and whisk in ½ cup hot soup. Return this mixture to soup, add salt, and continue to simmer for another 10 minutes. Serve sprinkled with paprika and minced parsley.

Serves 6.

Garlic Soup

1 cup peeled garlic, minced (about 24–30 cloves)
1 tablespoon onion, chopped
2 tablespoons olive oil
⅔ cup drained canned tomatoes
1 quart vegetable bouillon
Pepper
1 egg, slightly beaten
Croutons (see page 103)

Combine garlic and onion in a bowl. Heat oil in a large saucepan, add garlic and onion, and sauté until soft but not brown. Add tomatoes and stir in well. When tomatoes begin to lose their shape, add vegetable bouillon and pepper to taste; simmer for 15 minutes. Stir in egg, adding it very slowly, and serve at once, with croutons.

Serves 6.

Gazpacho

4 large tomatoes (1¾ pound), peeled
1 large cucumber, pared and halved
1 medium onion, peeled and halved
1 medium green pepper, seeded and quartered

1 pimiento, drained
2 12-ounce cans tomato juice
⅓ cup olive or salad oil
⅓ cup red wine vinegar
⅛ teaspoon Tabasco (hot pepper sauce)
Dash coarsely ground black pepper
2 cloves garlic, split
½ cup croutons (see page 103)
¼ cup chopped chives

In blender, combine 1 tomato, ½ cucumber, ½ onion, ¼ green pepper, the pimiento, and ½ cup tomato juice. Blend, covered, at high speed for 30 seconds to purée vegetables.

In a large bowl, mix puréed vegetables with remaining tomato juice, ¼ cup olive oil, the vinegar, Tabasco, and pepper. Refrigerate mixture, covered, until it is well chilled—at least 2 hours.

Prepare croutons. Chop separately remaining tomato, cucumber, onion, and green pepper. Place each of these and croutons in separate bowls to serve as accompaniments.

Just before serving, crush garlic and add to chilled soup, mixing well. Sprinkle with chopped chives. Serve gazpacho in chilled bowls.

Makes 6 servings.

Cream of Leek, Potato, and Tomato Soup

4 medium leeks
6 boiling potatoes
3 medium tomatoes
2 medium yellow onions
5 tablespoons butter
4 cups Vegetable Bouillon (recipe on page 95)
2 teaspoons white sugar
Salt

Pepper
1 pint heavy cream
Milk
Croutons (see page 103)
Parsley

Split and wash leeks thoroughly, then, using only the white part, cut in ½-inch chunks. Peel and dice potatoes. Coarsely chunk tomatoes. Peel and thinly slice onions. In a 3-quart soup pot over medium heat, melt 3 tablespoons butter. Add leeks and onion slices before butter starts bubbling. Adjust heat so that leeks and onions do not fry or brown, just gently simmer. In about 5 minutes, when leeks and onions are soft, add tomatoes, stir, and continue gently simmering. In a separate saucepan bring bouillon to boiling point. When tomatoes are just beginning to disintegrate, add potatoes, and then add boiling bouillon. Stir in sugar, salt, and pepper to taste. Turn heat down to a gentle simmer, then cover and cook until potatoes are completely soft. Cool; then blend mixture or pass it through a fine-mesh food mill. Put into refrigerator where it will thicken to a paste. (It can keep for several days.)

About 2 hours before serving, remove soup from refrigerator and let come to room temperature.

About 20 minutes before serving, gently reheat soup. As it is simmering, blend in 1 cup cream, using a wooden spoon and carefully scraping bottom of pan to make sure potatoes don't stick. Taste and adjust seasoning as necessary. For a more velvety texture, add cream, dash by dash. To thin it, add milk. When soup is just right, serve with croutons and chopped parsley.

Serves 6 to 8.

Minestrone

1 cup dried navy beans
5 cups water
Freshly ground pepper

¼ cup olive oil
1 cup finely chopped onion
½ cup chopped celery
1 clove garlic, finely minced
1 19-ounce can tomatoes
½ cup finely chopped parsley or cilantro
1 cup finely chopped cabbage
2 zucchini, trimmed but unpeeled, cut into ¼-inch cubes
8 ounces macaroni
Freshly grated Parmesan cheese

Place beans in a mixing bowl and add water to cover to the depth of 1 inch. Soak overnight.

Drain and empty beans into a kettle. Add 5 cups water and pepper to taste. Bring to a boil and simmer until tender, about 1 hour.

Heat oil in a skillet and cook onion and celery until wilted. Add garlic, and stir this mixture into beans. Add tomatoes and half the parsley, and simmer 20 minutes. Add cabbage, zucchini, and macaroni, and cook about 15 minutes longer, until macaroni is tender. Add remaining parsley and, if desired, a little more freshly chopped garlic. Serve with Parmesan cheese.

Makes 6 cups.

Sherry-Mushroom Soup

1 large onion, sliced
3 tablespoons butter
1 pound mushrooms, sliced
8 cups water
6 carrots, cubed
2 potatoes, cubed
Salt
Pepper
6 tablespoons sherry

Sauté onion in butter until light golden brown. Add mushrooms and continue to sauté for 3–4 minutes. Put water in a saucepan, and add carrots, potatoes, salt, and pepper. Cook for about 15 minutes over medium heat. Add mushrooms and onions, lower heat, and simmer for about 1 hour. Add sherry before serving.

Serves 8.

Onion Soup

2 cups chopped onions
¼ cup safflower oil
4 cloves garlic, minced
5 cups Vegetable Bouillon (recipe on page 95) or water
½ cup white wine
¼ cup tamari
8 ounces tofu
¼ cup olive oil
Grated Parmesan cheese

Preheat oven to 350°.

In a soup pot, cook onions slowly in the safflower oil until soft and transparent. Add half the garlic and cook for 3 minutes. Add bouillon or water, white wine, and tamari. Simmer for 45 minutes.

Slice tofu into ¼-inch slices. Mix together olive oil and remaining garlic. Baste tofu slices with this mixture; then bake on an oiled baking sheet for 20 minutes or until crusty.

After soup has simmered, ladle it into individual ovenproof bowls. Top with a piece of tofu sprinkled with Parmesan cheese. Broil until cheese is golden brown. Serve immediately.

Serves 6.

Pasta i Fagioli

1 pound dried white pinto beans
¼ cup olive oil
½ yellow onion, finely chopped
2 celery hearts (with tops), finely chopped
½ carrot, finely chopped
3 tablespoons tomato paste
1 clove garlic, chopped
1 teaspoon oregano
½ cup white wine
1 pound fettuccine, broken into small pieces
Pepper

Soak beans overnight. Rinse and bring to boil in a large pot or Dutch oven, using enough water to cover beans by 1–2 inches. Add 1 tablespoon oil to beans as they cook. Cook beans until al dente, about 35–45 minutes.

In a medium skillet, heat remaining 2 tablespoons oil, add onion, celery, and carrot, and sauté until vegetables are just beginning to get tender. Add tomato paste, garlic, oregano, and white wine. Cover, and let simmer for a few minutes. Add this mixture to beans. Season with pepper to taste, bring soup to boil, then lower flame and simmer for 5 minutes.

Cook fettuccine in 1½ quarts boiling water until very al dente. Drain well. Add pasta to beans. Simmer 5–6 minutes. Garnish with fresh ground pepper.

Serves 6 to 8.

Split Pea Soup

2 cups split peas
10 cups water
2 tablespoons oil
1 cup carrots, finely chopped
1 cup celery, finely chopped

1 cup onion, finely chopped
2 cloves garlic, minced
½ teaspoon marjoram
½ teaspoon basil
¼ teaspoon cumin
½ teaspoon pepper
2 tablespoons butter
Pinch cayenne pepper

Put split peas in a pot with water, bring to a boil, then lower heat and simmer for 1 hour. Skim off foam.

Sauté vegetables in oil for about 5 minutes, then add remaining ingredients except cayenne pepper and butter, and sauté another 5 minutes.

Add vegetable mixture to split peas, and simmer, stirring occasionally, for about 45 minutes.

Add butter and cayenne pepper, and serve very hot.

Serves 6 to 8.

Creamed Spinach Soup

1 pound fresh spinach
2 tablespoons minced green onion
1 garlic clove, minced
3 tablespoons butter
Pinch of nutmeg
5 cups Vegetable Bouillon (see recipe page 95)
1 cup heavy cream
Salt
Pepper
4 tablespoons butter (½ stick), cut into bits
Parsley

Wash spinach thoroughly, removing all sand. Sauté spinach, onion, and garlic in butter, stirring frequently, until spinach is wilted. Add nutmeg and bouillon, cover, bring to a boil, and then lower heat and simmer for 30 minutes. Remove from heat, allow to cool slightly, and purée mixture in a blender.

Return mixture to soup pot, add cream, salt and pepper to taste. Swirl in butter bits, cook 5 or 10 minutes, then serve topped with parsley.

Serves 6.

Sweet Potato Soup

1¼ pounds sweet potatoes
3 carrots
1 large stalk celery
1 bay leaf
6 cups water
2 tablespoons lemon juice
1 teaspoon paprika
1½ tablespoons butter
½ cup heavy cream

Peel sweet potatoes and cut in small dice. Scrape and thinly slice carrots. Slice celery. Put vegetables and bay leaf in a pot with water. Bring to a boil, then lower heat and let soup simmer for about 1 hour, stirring occasionally. Before serving, add lemon juice, paprika, butter, and cream, and continue to cook for 2–3 minutes, stirring constantly. Remove bay leaf before serving.

Serves 6.

Clear Vegetable Bouillon

4 quarts water
1 head cabbage, quartered
6 carrots

4 medium leeks
6 boiling potatoes
4 white turnips
1 cup dried split peas
1 small bunch parsley
1 tablespoon whole caraway seed
Salt
Pepper

In a large soup pot, heat 4 quarts water to boil. Cut cabbage into quarters; scrape carrots and cut into chunks; split and carefully wash leeks to remove all sand, then cut into chunks. Peel potatoes and turnips and cut into chunks. Add potatoes, turnips, cabbage, carrots, and leeks to water, along with split peas, a handful of parsley, caraway, salt, and pepper. When liquid returns to a boil, turn down flame and simmer, uncovered, for at least 2 hours, longer if possible. When cooking is finished, remove, squeeze out, and throw away vegetables. Strain out smaller particles through a fine-mesh sieve. The resulting rich and potent broth will keep perfectly in a refrigerator.

Makes about 3 quarts.

Vichyssoise

1½ cups chopped, peeled raw potato
1½ cups chopped leek (white part only)
1½ cups Vegetable Bouillon (recipe on page 95) or water
1 cup milk
1 cup heavy cream
½ teaspoon salt
Dash pepper
Pinch dill
2 tablespoons chopped chives

In large saucepan, combine potatoes, leeks, and bouillon or water. Bring to boil. Reduce heat and simmer, covered, for 25 minutes. Vegetables should be very soft.

Blend vegetables in food processor or blender 1–2 minutes or until smooth. Turn into large bowl. Refrigerate, covered, until chilled—about 3 hours.

Stir in milk, cream, salt, pepper, and dill until blended. Serve topped with chives.

Serves 6.

Salads

Avocado Salad with Crème Fraîche and Raspberry Vinegar Dressing

1 pound very large mushrooms or 4 fresh shiitake
   mushrooms, very thinly sliced
2 avocados, peeled and very thinly sliced
Watercress sprigs

Dressing
2½ cups crème fraîche (recipe below)
¼ cup (scant) raspberry vinegar (recipe below) or red wine
   vinegar
Salt
Freshly ground white pepper

Arrange mushrooms and avocado slices on individual salad plates.

Combine ingredients for dressing and pour around salad. Garnish with watercress sprigs.

Serves 6.

To make *crème fraîche*, combine 1 part sour cream with 2 parts whipping cream and heat to 110°. Let stand at room temperature until thickened, about 8 hours.

For *raspberry vinegar*, add about 12 fresh or unsweetened frozen raspberries to 2 cups red wine vinegar and let stand at room temperature for at least 1 week before using.

Cuban Avocado Salad

4 tablespoons fresh lime juice
1½ cups mayonnaise (see page 158)
2 large avocados, chilled, peeled, and diced
1 medium pineapple, chilled, peeled, and diced
Crisp lettuce leaves

Blend together lime juice and mayonnaise, and chill for 1 hour.
Arrange cubes of avocado and pineapple on lettuce leaves, and
pour dressing over them. Serve at once.

Serves 6.

Stuffed Avocado

3 avocados
3 tablespoons lemon juice
3 firm, ripe tomatoes, peeled, seeded, and diced
6 scallions, minced
4 tablespoons olive oil
1½ tablespoons vinegar
1½ teaspoons sugar
1 tablespoon chopped pimiento
1 green chili, chopped
⅓ cup mayonnaise
Parsley

Cut avocados lengthwise, remove pits, and peel. Brush exposed surfaces with lemon juice to prevent discoloration.
Combine all other ingredients except mayonnaise and parsley,
and fill avocado halves with mixture. Garnish top of each with a
dollop of mayonnaise and a sprig of parsley. Chill before
serving.

Serves 6.

Beet Salad

3 pounds washed, unpeeled beets (leave roots and 4
   inches of stem intact)
Water
2 teaspoons caraway seed
2 teaspoons whole cloves
3 cups cider vinegar
⅔ cup sugar
½ cup water
3 sprigs fresh dill or ½ teaspoon dried dill

Preheat oven to 350°.

Put beets in a casserole with water to cover, and boil for 15–20
minutes or until almost tender. Drain off all but 1 cup water.
Cover casserole and bake beets for 30 minutes. Let beets stand
until cool enough to handle, then trim off stems and carefully
peel beets. Slice beets thinly. Put slices in a bowl, and sprinkle
with caraway seed and whole cloves.

In a saucepan combine vinegar, sugar, ½ cup water, and dill,
and boil mixture for 5 minutes or until sugar is dissolved.
Strain mixture over beets and let it cool.

Chill salad before serving. It will keep indefinitely in the refrigerator and improve with time.

Makes 4 cups.

Beet and Endive Salad

⅓ cup whipping cream
1 teaspoon Dijon mustard
1 teaspoon fresh lemon juice
Freshly ground pepper
2 Belgian endives, cut crosswise into 1-inch slices
6 mushrooms, sliced
2 cooked beets, chilled, peeled, and cut in julienne strips

1 green onion, chopped
Lettuce leaves
Minced fresh parsley

Combine cream, mustard, lemon juice, and pepper; whisk until thick.

Combine endives and mushrooms in a small bowl. Add 3 table-spoons dressing and toss well. Mix beets, onion, and remaining dressing in another bowl.

Line 2 salad plates with lettuce. Spoon endive mixture over lettuce and top with beet mixture. Sprinkle with parsley.

Serves 6.

Caesar Salad

2 heads romaine lettuce
1 cup olive oil
¼ cup wine vinegar
Juice of 1 lemon
1 egg, coddled for about ½ minute in hot water
¾ cup Parmesan cheese
Croutons (recipe opposite page)

Wash and tear lettuce, and place in a large serving bowl. Combine oil, vinegar, and lemon juice in a smaller bowl and mix thoroughly. (For effect, this dressing can be prepared at table.) Break coddled egg onto top of lettuce, add Parmesan cheese and croutons, and toss until egg is fairly well absorbed and leaves are coated with egg-cheese mixture. Add dressing, toss thoroughly, and serve.

Serves 6 to 8.

Croutons

4 tablespoons butter
1 tablespoon oil
3 cloves garlic, chopped
6 slices whole-wheat bread, toasted and cut into cubes

Melt butter in a large skillet. Add oil and garlic. Place lightly toasted bread cubes into skillet, and sauté over very low heat, turning each cube constantly until it is thoroughly soaked with butter-garlic mixture and lightly browned. Remove with tongs and drain on a paper towel.

Cucumber and Cheese Salad

¾ cup sour cream
3 tablespoons chopped fresh dill
2 tablespoons vinegar
1 tablespoon chopped chives
1 tablespoon olive oil
1 garlic clove, crushed
⅛ teaspoon cayenne pepper
4 cucumbers, peeled and cut into ½-inch dice
¼ pound Swiss cheese, coarsely chopped
6 scallions, thinly sliced
6 radishes, thinly sliced
4 hard-boiled eggs, chopped
¼ cup minced parsley
1 tablespoon tarragon vinegar
Pepper

In a small bowl combine sour cream, chopped fresh dill, 2 tablespoons vinegar, chopped chives, olive oil, garlic, and cayenne pepper, and chill dressing. In a salad bowl combine cucumbers, Swiss cheese, scallions, radishes, hard-boiled eggs, and parsley. Sprinkle mixture with 1 tablespoon tarragon vinegar, tossing lightly, add pepper to taste, and chill salad for at least 2 hours. Pour dressing over salad and toss.

Serves 6 to 8.

Cucumber Salad with Paprika Dressing

4 medium cucumbers
2 teaspoons salt
⅓ cup white wine vinegar
1 small onion, thinly sliced
2 teaspoons sweet paprika
1 teaspoon dillseed
½ teaspoon sugar
½ teaspoon white pepper

Combine all ingredients except cucumbers and salt in a bowl and let stand for at least 30 minutes.

Peel, halve lengthwise, and seed cucumbers. Slice cucumbers thinly, toss with salt in a colander, and let drain for at least 15 minutes.

Dry cucumbers with paper towels, and toss with dressing. Chill before serving.

Serves 6.

Delmonico Salad

1 large head romaine lettuce
7 tablespoons olive oil
3 tablespoons vinegar
2 tablespoons heavy cream
3 tablespoons crumbled Roquefort cheese
Tabasco (hot pepper sauce)
1 hard-boiled egg, finely chopped

Wash and dry lettuce, then cut out thick spine from each leaf. Tear leaves and place in a plastic bag in refrigerator until ready to use.

Combine olive oil, vinegar, cream, and crumbled cheese in a bowl, and whisk until smooth. Add a couple of dashes of Tabasco and chopped egg.

Mix dressing and chilled lettuce in a large bowl and serve.

Serves 6.

Greek-Style Salad

6 medium tomatoes, sliced
¼ pound feta cheese, crumbled
1 small onion, thinly sliced
1 3½-ounce can pitted ripe olives, drained and sliced
½ cup olive or salad oil
⅓ cup red wine vinegar
2 tablespoons minced parsley
4 teaspoons sugar
½ teaspoon basil
¼ teaspoon cracked pepper
Lettuce leaves

About 2½ hours before serving, place tomato slices, feta cheese, onion, and olives in a 13″ × 9″ baking dish; set aside.

In a small bowl, with a fork, mix oil, vinegar, parsley, sugar, basil, and pepper. Pour dressing over tomato mixture; with a rubber spatula, gently lift tomato slices to coat with dressing. Cover baking dish, and refrigerate at least 2 hours to blend flavors.

To serve, line a chilled platter with lettuce leaves. Arrange tomato mixture on lettuce.

Serves 8.

Mozzarella, Tomato, and Fresh Basil Salad

6 large beefsteak tomatoes, each cut into 4–6 slices
**12 ounces fresh Mozzarella cheese, cut into same number of
   slices as tomatoes**
¼–½ cup olive oil

2 tablespoons wine vinegar
Fresh basil (leaves of 1 large bunch)
Freshly ground pepper

Divide tomatoes and cheese into 4 equal portions. Arrange 1 slice of cheese over each tomato slice. Blend oil, vinegar, and basil leaves in blender or food processor. Spread thin layer of basil mixture (pesto) over cheese. Continue layering in same order for each portion, ending with pesto. Arrange in a circle on a platter, overlapping slightly. Serve at room temperature.

Pass olive oil and pepper separately.

Serves 6.

Mushroom-Nut Salad

½ pound fresh mushrooms, sliced
¾ cup olive or salad oil
½ cup wine vinegar
2 tablespoons water
¾ teaspoon salt
¼ teaspoon onion powder
1 small head romaine lettuce, torn into bite-size chunks
¾ cup toasted filberts, chopped (walnuts or pecans may be
    substituted) (see below)
¾ teaspoon savory
⅛ teaspoon pepper

Combine mushrooms, oil, vinegar, water, and seasonings in a bowl. Chill about 1 hour.

To toast filberts, spread nuts in shallow pan and bake in 400° oven for 10–15 minutes, stirring occasionally.

Toss undrained mushrooms with lettuce and filberts in salad bowl.

Makes 6 to 8 servings.

Sweet and Sour Spinach Salad

4 egg yolks
1 teaspoon dry mustard
¼ teaspoon freshly ground white pepper
½ cup olive oil
¼ cup sugar
3 tablespoons red wine vinegar
Juice of ½ lemon
1 pound spinach (stems discarded), torn into pieces
12 white mushrooms, thinly sliced

Beat egg yolks in small bowl until light and lemon colored. Add mustard and pepper, and blend. Whisking constantly, add olive oil drop by drop at first, then in a slow, steady stream, until thickened. Stir in sugar, vinegar, and lemon juice, and mix well.

Place spinach in large salad bowl. Add mushrooms and dressing; toss.

Serves 6 to 8.

String Bean Purée

3 medium onions, sliced fine
3 tablespoons oil
3 hard-boiled eggs, grated
2½ cups cooked string beans
½ cup walnuts
2 tablespoons mayonnaise
Salt
Pepper
½ teaspoon celery seed
Juice of ½–1 whole lemon (to taste)
Grated egg yolk, chopped parsley, or chopped scallions
Lettuce leaves

Sauté onions in oil. Allow to brown, but do not burn. Remove from pan and pour into mixing bowl along with pan oil. Add grated eggs, and mash onions and eggs together.

In blender, purée beans, nuts, mayonnaise, salt, pepper, and celery seed. Pour into egg-onion mixture and blend, stirring in lemon juice to taste. Garnish with grated egg yolk, chopped parsley, or chopped scallions. Serve on lettuce leaves as a salad.

Serves 4.

Tomatoes Stuffed with Cucumbers

6 ripe medium tomatoes
Salt
Pepper
½ cup sour cream
1 teaspoon Worcestershire sauce
½ teaspoon salt
¼ teaspoon lemon juice
2 cucumbers, peeled, seeded, and cut into ½-inch cubes
Chopped dill

Cut off the top quarter of tomatoes and scoop out pulp; sprinkle shells lightly with salt and pepper. Invert tomatoes on a rack and let drain for 30 minutes.

In a bowl combine sour cream, Worcestershire sauce, ½ teaspoon salt, lemon juice, and pepper to taste. Stir in cucumbers. Fill tomato cases with cucumber mixture and sprinkle with chopped dill.

Serves 6.

Main Dishes

Corn Fritters

3 eggs, separated, at room temperature
3 cups fresh corn kernels cut off the cob (about 2 ears)
1 teaspoon salt
¼ teaspoon pepper
¼ cup sifted all-purpose flour
¼ teaspoon baking powder
½ cup vegetable oil
Honey

In a medium-size bowl, beat egg yolks well. Add corn, salt, pepper, flour, and baking powder. Mix well.

In another bowl, beat egg whites until stiff but not dry. Fold egg whites into corn mixture.

In a large skillet heat oil over moderately high heat. Drop batter by rounded tablespoonfuls into the skillet. Fry 3–5 minutes, until lightly browned. Turn and brown the other side. Drain on paper towels.

Serve warm topped with honey.

Makes 6 to 8 servings.

Eggplant Cordon Bleu with Creamy Tomato Sauce

2 medium eggplants, peeled and sliced into ¼-inch slices
1 pound Swiss cheese, sliced into julienne strips
3 eggs, beaten
2 cups bread crumbs
4 tablespoons butter

Preheat oven to 350°.

Place eggplants, weighted, in colander to drain. Melt butter in skillet, then dip eggplant slices in eggs and bread crumbs and sauté lightly on each side until just golden and still pliant. Pat excess butter off sautéed eggplant and place 3 or 4 strips of cheese on each slice. Roll up eggplant around cheese, and place rolled slices in a large casserole. Bake for 15 minutes. Remove and serve in individual casseroles, topped with Creamy Tomato Sauce and chopped parsley.

Creamy Tomato Sauce

4 medium tomatoes, or 1 16-ounce can
3 teaspoons olive oil
1 clove garlic, unpeeled but crushed
2 shallots, peeled and sliced
1 teaspoon tomato paste
1 cup heavy cream
½ cup chopped celery
½ teaspoon dried basil
1 bay leaf

Peel, seed, and chop tomatoes. (If using canned tomatoes, discard liquid.) Heat oil in a saucepan and add garlic and shallots. Stir in tomato pulp, tomato paste, celery, basil, and bay leaf. Stir in cream, cover saucepan, and simmer sauce for 20 minutes. Remove from heat, remove bay leaf, and pour sauce into a blender. Blend until sauce is smooth.

Eggplant Enchiladas

1 cup chopped onion
2 medium cloves garlic, crushed
2–3 tablespoons olive oil for sautéeing vegetables
1½ teaspoon salt
6 cups cubed eggplant (approximately 2 small eggplants)
1 cup chopped green pepper
1 cup chopped, toasted almonds
Lots of black pepper
1 packed cup grated mild, white cheese
Vegetable oil for frying tortillas (see page 170)
12 tortillas

Preheat oven to 350°.

Sauté onion and garlic in olive oil in a large skillet. Add salt. Cook over medium heat, stirring occasionally, for about 5 minutes. Add eggplant (cut into ½-inch cubes). Mix. Cover and cook about 10 minutes, or until eggplant is soft. Add green pepper, almonds, and black pepper. Cook another 5 minutes, stirring frequently. Remove from heat and add cheese. Mix.

Heat vegetable oil in a heavy skillet. Fry each tortilla on both sides—only 10 seconds on each side (must be soft for rolling). Drain.

Fill each tortilla by placing about ¼ cup filling on one side and rolling it up. Place filled enchiladas gently in a baking pan. Pour hot sauce over top. Place in oven and bake about 20 minutes.

Serves 6 (2 enchiladas per serving).

Ginger-Stuffed Eggplant

6 medium eggplants
2 onions, peeled and chopped
Oil
Tamari

¼ cup grated fresh ginger
9 stalks celery, thinly sliced
3 red peppers, thinly sliced
6 tablespoons chunky peanut butter
1 teaspoon curry powder
Dash cayenne pepper
Dash nutmeg
Grapes

Preheat oven to 350°.

Cut eggplants in half lengthwise. Hollow out shells to ⅛ inch and set aside. Cube eggplant pulp. Sauté onions and eggplant cubes in oil until both are tender. Add a few teaspoons of tamari to taste.

In a large bowl, mix eggplant mixture with ginger, celery, red peppers, peanut butter, curry powder, cayenne pepper, and nutmeg. Place mixture in eggplant shells and bake for 45 minutes.

Garnish each eggplant half with a small bunch of green grapes.

Serves 6 as a main course or 12 as an appetizer or side dish.

Eggplant Newburg

¼ cup butter
½ pound whole mushrooms
1 large eggplant, peeled and cubed
3 tablespoons chopped onion
3 tablespoons sherry
2 tablespoons butter
2 tablespoons flour
2 cups light cream, or 1 cup cream and 1 cup milk, heated
2 egg yolks
2 tablespoons water
Nutmeg
Cayenne pepper
Toast

In a skillet, melt ¼ cup butter. Add whole mushrooms, egg-plant cubes, and onion, and sauté until almost tender. Add sherry and simmer 1–2 minutes.

In another, smaller skillet, heat 2 tablespoons butter and combine with flour to make a roux. Add heated cream and stir with a whisk until mixture thickens. Beat egg yolks with water, and blend into white sauce. Pour sauce over mushroom mixture in pan, and stir well, seasoning with some grated nutmeg, and just a touch of cayenne pepper. Serve immediately over toast.

Makes 5 servings.

Cold Eggplant Provençale

3 large eggplants, sliced into ½-inch-thick rounds
Salt
1 cup chopped fresh parsley
2 large onions, thinly sliced
6 large tomatoes, peeled and sliced
2 large garlic cloves, minced
2 celery hearts, finely chopped
2 teaspoons black currants
1 teaspoon dried basil
1 teaspoon crushed black peppercorns
1 teaspoon chopped capers
Freshly ground pepper
1 cup olive oil
Lemon wedges (optional)

Sprinkle eggplant slices generously on both sides with salt. Place in large colander, cover with weight, and let stand about 45 minutes. Rinse thoroughly under cold running water and pat dry with paper towels.

Preheat oven to 275°.

Arrange half of eggplant in 11" × 15" baking dish. Sprinkle with half the parsley. Arrange onions, tomatoes, garlic, celery, currants, basil, peppercorns, and capers evenly on top. Season to taste with salt and pepper, and sprinkle with remaining parsley. Top with remaining eggplant, and pour olive oil evenly over the dish. Cover tightly with foil and bake 4 hours. Remove foil and stir mixture well with long fork or spoon. Continue baking 1 hour. Let cool, then chill.

Let stand at room temperature 2–3 hours before serving. Garnish with lemon wedges.

Serves 10 to 12.

Huevos Rancheros

6 tortillas (see page 170)
3 tablespoons butter, divided
3 medium onions, chopped
3 cloves garlic, minced
2 green peppers, chopped
3 tomatoes, chopped
1 chili pepper, chopped
6 eggs
1 head romaine lettuce, shredded
6 ounces Cheddar cheese, shredded

Preheat oven to 350°.

Wrap tortillas in foil and place on top rack of oven. In a large skillet, sauté onions, garlic, and green peppers in 1½ tablespoons of butter, stirring often. When onions are transparent, add tomatoes and chili pepper, and continue cooking for about 2 or 3 minutes. Transfer vegetables to bowl. Melt remaining butter in skillet and fry eggs until whites are just firm. Remove tortillas from oven and place one on each plate. Top with shredded lettuce, then an egg. Spoon vegetable mixture on top of eggs and sprinkle each with cheese.

Serves 6.

Lima Bean Loaf

1 cup dry lima beans
¼ cup butter
1 small onion, chopped
1 cup thinly sliced celery
⅓ cup flour
1 cup milk
1 egg, beaten
1 cup soft, fine whole-wheat bread crumbs
1½ cups chopped raw carrots
1 teaspoon salt
¼ teaspoon pepper
1½ cup chopped peanuts
Cheddar cheese slices

Soak beans overnight in cold water. Drain, rinse, and cook in water to cover until tender, about 1½ hours. Drain beans and mash.

Preheat oven to 375°.

Melt butter in saucepan, add onion, and sauté about 3 minutes. Add celery, cover, and cook until tender. Add flour and cook 2 minutes. Add milk, stirring until thickened.

Remove from heat and stir in beaten egg. Add bread crumbs, carrots, salt, pepper, and peanuts.

Spoon mixture into greased 8" × 4" loaf pan and bake for 35–45 minutes. Arrange cheese slices over loaf and bake until cheese melts.

Makes 6 servings.

Mushrooms Polonaise

1½ pounds mushrooms, sliced
1 onion, chopped
¾ cup butter

2 tablespoons flour
1 cup sour cream
1 cup heavy cream
½ teaspoon nutmeg
Pepper
½ cup parsley, chopped
¼ cup bread crumbs

Preheat oven to 350°.

Place mushrooms and onion in a heavy, *dry* skillet. Cover, and over very low heat, allow vegetables to cook in their own juices until they almost stick to the pan. Add ½ cup butter. When butter has melted, add flour and cook, stirring constantly, for 5 minutes over very low heat. Stir in sour cream and heavy cream with a wooden spoon, then add nutmeg and pepper to taste. Continue to cook, uncovered, until mixture has thickened. Stir in parsley.

In another pan, lightly sauté bread crumbs in ¼ cup butter. Pour mushroom mixture into a buttered, shallow casserole. Sprinkle top with sautéed bread crumbs. Bake until mixture has set and bread crumbs have browned a little more.

Serves 6.

Mushroom Stew

5 tablespoons butter
1 tablespoon olive oil
2 bay leaves
2 cloves garlic, minced
1 large yellow onion, chopped
2 tablespoons flour
1 cup vegetable bouillon
1 cup tomato juice
2 cups peeled, quartered tomatoes
1 teaspoon basil
1 teaspoon thyme

1½ pounds mushrooms, washed
1 pound boiling onions
Red wine to taste
Chopped fresh parsley to taste
Pepper

In a medium saucepan, melt 2 tablespoons butter with 1 table-spoon olive oil and add to it bay leaves, garlic, and yellow onion. Sauté until onion is golden. Stir in flour, and lower heat. Cook this roux for several minutes, stirring constantly, and then add vegetable bouillon and tomato juice. Stir with a whisk, and add tomatoes.

In another, larger pot, melt remaining 3 tablespoons butter, and add basil, thyme, and mushrooms. Sauté mushrooms over high heat for several minutes, turning often. Add boiling onions and tomato sauce. Turn down heat and simmer stew for about 20 minutes. Add a little red wine, some chopped parsley, and pepper to taste. Cook a few more minutes. Remove bay leaves. Serve hot.

Serves 6.

Rice with Beans and Cheese

2 cups brown rice, cooked
2 cups cooked black beans
3 cloves garlic, minced
1 large onion, chopped
½ cup canned chilies, chopped
½ pound Jack cheese, shredded
½ pound Ricotta cheese, thinned slightly with milk
½ cup Cheddar cheese, grated

Preheat oven to 350°.

Mix rice, beans, garlic, onion, and chilies. Layer this mixture alternately in a greased casserole with Jack and Ricotta cheese.

End with rice mixture. Bake for 30 minutes. During last few minutes of baking, sprinkle grated Cheddar cheese over top.

Serves 6 to 8.

Sweet Shepherd's Pie

1 pound broccoli
1 bunch spinach
1 onion, coarsely chopped
2 tablespoons oil
1 green pepper, diced
1 pound (4 medium) carrots, diced
½ teaspoon basil
1 bay leaf
¾ cup chopped fresh tomatoes
3 cups mashed sweet potatoes (4 medium potatoes mashed
   with ¼ cup milk and
   1 tablespoon butter)
Paprika

Preheat oven to 350°.

Cut broccoli into flowerets and stems. Peel and slice stems in ¼-inch rounds. Wash spinach thoroughly and tear.

Sauté onion in oil. Add broccoli, green pepper, and carrots; then add basil and bay leaf. Stir well and add tomatoes. Bring to a boil, cover, turn heat to low, and simmer for 15 minutes or until vegetables are just tender. Stir in spinach. Drain off excess liquid and put vegetables into a 9" × 13" baking dish. Spread potatoes over top and bake for 10–15 minutes, until potatoes are piping hot. Shake paprika over top before serving.

Serves 4 to 6.

Baked Tofu Mozzarella

1 cup whole-wheat bread crumbs
½ tablespoon basil
½ tablespoon oregano
2 eggs
1 tablespoon tamari or soy sauce
2 cloves garlic, minced
1½ pounds tofu
Flour for dredging
2 cups commercial tomato sauce
Sautéed mushrooms or chopped black olives (optional)
8 ounces grated Mozzarella cheese

Preheat oven to 375°.

In a small bowl, combine bread crumbs, basil, and oregano. In another small bowl, beat eggs with soy sauce and garlic.

Pat tofu dry with paper towels and cut cake into 4 triangles. Dredge each triangle in flour, then dip in egg mixture and then into bread crumbs. Place coated triangles on a baking sheet. Bake at 375° for 20 minutes or until golden and crisp.

Remove from oven and place tofu triangles in a greased casserole. Cover with tomato sauce, sautéed mushrooms, chopped black olives, and grated Mozzarella cheese. Bake again until cheese melts, then serve.

Serves 6.

Garden Tomato Bake

8 medium tomatoes, peeled and quartered
Salt
Pepper
1 teaspoon sugar
½ teaspoon dry mustard
2 large onions, sliced

2 tablespoons butter
2½ cups fresh bread crumbs
6 tablespoons butter, melted
¼ cup grated Parmesan cheese

Preheat oven to 350°.

Mix tomatoes, salt, pepper, sugar, and dry mustard until blended well. Sauté onions in 2 tablespoons butter until just translucent. Mix bread crumbs with 6 tablespoons melted butter until blended well. In a buttered 1½-quart casserole, layer tomatoes, onions, and crumbs. Bake for 20–30 minutes. Sprinkle with cheese, bake 5 more minutes, and serve.

Serves 6.

Vegetarian Casserole

1 large eggplant
2 medium zucchini
4 tablespoons olive oil
2 large onions, chopped
1 large carrot, grated
3 cups canned Italian-style tomatoes
2 tablespoons minced parsley
2 tablespoons minced dillweed
2 garlic cloves, minced
1 tablespoon Worcestershire sauce
Salt
Pepper
1 cup fresh green beans, trimmed and broken into pieces
2 cups cooked kidney beans or large white lima beans
2 tablespoons bread crumbs
3 tablespoons grated Parmesan cheese
2 tablespoons butter, cut into small pieces
Sour cream

Cut unpeeled eggplant and zucchini into ⅓-inch slices. Place eggplant slices and zucchini slices in separate colanders, cover with salt, and drain, letting stand at room temperature for 1–2 hours. After draining, squeeze out as much liquid as possible from eggplant and zucchini.

Preheat oven to 325°.

In a large frying pan, heat oil, then add onions and cook, stirring constantly, for 3–5 minutes, or until soft. Do not brown. Add grated carrot and tomatoes. Cook over low-to-medium heat, stirring frequently, until sauce is thick and soft. Add parsley, dill, garlic, and Worcestershire sauce, and cook for 2 more minutes.

In a buttered 2-quart baking dish or casserole, make alternate layers of tomato sauce and all other vegetables, beginning and ending with sauce. Combine bread crumbs and cheese and sprinkle on top of casserole. Dot with butter. Bake for about 1 hour, or until top is golden and bubbly. Serve hot, with a bowl of sour cream on the side.

Serves 6.

Fresh Vegetable Crêpes

5 medium zucchini
3 medium yellow straightneck squash
2 medium red or green peppers
1 medium onion
8 eggs
Water
Oil
½ teaspoon oregano leaves
⅛ teaspoon pepper
8-ounces Cheddar cheese, shredded

Slice zucchini and yellow squash lengthwise in half; cut each half crosswise into ¼-inch slices. Cut peppers into thin strips. Dice onion.

In medium bowl, beat eggs and ½ cup water with fork until well blended. In 6- or 7-inch crêpe pan over medium heat, heat 1 teaspoon oil, tilting pan to grease sides. Pour ¼ cup egg mixture into skillet, tilting to make a thin crêpe. When top of crêpe is set and underside is delicately browned, run spatula around side and bottom to loosen; slide crêpe onto plate. Repeat to make 11 more; keep warm.

In 12-inch skillet over medium heat, in ¼ cup hot oil, cook onion until tender and lightly browned, stirring occasionally. Add zucchini, yellow squash, red or green peppers, oregano, pepper, and ½ cup water; cook until all vegetables are tender, about 20 minutes, stirring frequently. Remove skillet from heat; stir in cheese until blended.

To serve, spread a heaping ⅓ cupful vegetable mixture onto center of each crêpe; fold two sides of crêpe over filling to make roll. Arrange filled crêpes on warm platter.

Serves 6.

Russian Vegetable Pie

Pastry
1¼ cups flour
1 teaspoon sugar
1 teaspoon salt
3 tablespoons butter
4 ounces softened cream cheese

Filling
1 head cabbage (about 3½–4 cups shredded)
½ pound mushrooms
1 yellow onion
3 tablespoons butter
⅛ teaspoon marjoram
¼ teaspoon tarragon
⅛ teaspoon basil
Pepper

4 ounces softened cream cheese
5 hard-boiled eggs
Dill

To make pastry, sift together dry ingredients, cutting in butter and working it together with cream cheese. Roll out ⅔ of pastry and line a 9-inch pie dish. Roll out remaining pastry and make a circle large enough to cover dish. Refrigerate pastry to chill.

Preheat oven to 400°.

Shred cabbage. Wash and slice mushrooms. Peel and chop onion.

In a large skillet, melt about 2 tablespoons butter. Add onion and cabbage, and sauté for several minutes, stirring constantly. Add marjoram, tarragon, basil, and pepper. Allow mixture to cook until cabbage is wilted and onion is soft, stirring frequently. Remove from pan and set aside.

Add another tablespoon of butter to the pan and sauté mushrooms lightly for 5–6 minutes, stirring constantly.

Spread softened cream cheese in bottom of pie shell. Slice eggs and arrange slices in a layer over cheese. Sprinkle with a little chopped dill, then cover with cabbage. Make a final layer of sautéed mushrooms and cover with the circle of pastry. Press pastry together tightly at the edges and flute them. With a sharp knife, cut a few short slashes through top crust.

Bake for 15 minutes, then turn temperature down to 350° and continue baking for another 20–25 minutes, or until crust is light brown.

Serves 6.

Vegetable Stroganoff

1 cup chopped onion
½ pound mushrooms, chopped
3 cups sour cream

1½ cups plain yogurt
½ teaspoon dillweed
Dash soy sauce
¼ teaspoon sweet paprika
6 cups chopped vegetables (broccoli, carrots, cauliflower,
    cabbage, peppers, cherry tomatoes, zucchini)
4 cups raw noodles
2 tablespoons butter
6 scallions, minced

Sauté onion and mushrooms in butter until the onion is soft but not brown. Combine onion, mushrooms, sour cream, yogurt, dillweed, soy sauce, and paprika in the top of a double boiler, and heat gently for about 30 minutes.

Steam vegetables until just barely tender.

Cook noodles in boiling water until tender. Drain and toss with butter.

Place the noodles on a large platter, ladle steamed vegetables atop noodles, pour sauce over vegetables and noodles, and garnish with minced scallions.

Serves 6.

Vegetable Soufflé with Tahini Sauce

Purée can be prepared 1–2 days ahead and refrigerated.

2 pounds turnips, peeled and shredded
2 pounds carrots, peeled and shredded
2 heads broccoli or cauliflower
6 tablespoons butter (¾ stick)
¼ cup firmly packed light brown sugar
2–3 tablespoons curry powder, or to taste
1 tablespoon onion powder
1 teaspoon salt
¼ teaspoon freshly ground pepper

⅛ teaspoon freshly grated nutmeg
⅔ cup bread crumbs
12 egg whites, at room temperature
Tahini Sauce (recipe below)

Steam turnips and carrots until just tender, 2–3 minutes. Drain well. Separate broccoli or cauliflower into flowerets, discarding most of stem. Steam until tender, about 5 minutes. Drain well. Purée vegetables in a food processor until smooth.

Melt 4 tablespoons butter and sugar in large skillet and sauté over low heat. Stir in seasonings and mix well. Add puréed vegetables and cook, stirring frequently, until excess moisture has evaporated, about 15 minutes. Let cool. Taste and adjust seasoning. (Can be prepared ahead to this point, covered and refrigerated. Bring to room temperature before proceeding.)

Position rack in lower third of oven, and preheat to 450°. Coat 9″ × 12″ pan or 3-quart round baking dish with 2 tablespoons butter. Sprinkle bottom of dish with half of bread crumbs.

Beat egg whites in large bowl until stiff but not dry. Stir about ⅓ of whites into purée and blend well. Gently fold in remaining whites. Turn into baking dish and sprinkle with remaining bread crumbs. Bake 15 minutes. Reduce temperature to 350° and continue baking until puffed and golden brown, about 30 minutes. Serve immediately, accompanied with Tahini Sauce.

Serves 20.

Tahini Sauce

½ cup tahini (sesame seed paste)
2 cups plain yogurt
2 garlic cloves
1 tablespoon fresh parsley
1 tablespoon chopped fresh dill
2 tablespoons fresh lemon juice
2 tablespoons currants or raisins (optional)

Stir tahini well so that oil is absorbed. Combine in processor with yogurt, garlic, parsley, and dill, and mix until smooth. Add lemon juice to thin slightly and mix another 30 seconds. Stir in currants or raisins if desired. Transfer to sauceboat, cover, and chill thoroughly.

Zucchini Loaf

3 cups shredded zucchini
1 cup cooked brown rice
1 cup wheat germ
1¼ cups shredded Cheddar cheese
1 cup chopped walnuts
2 cups sliced fresh mushrooms
4 green onions, sliced
4 eggs
1 teaspoon oregano
2–4 garlic cloves, minced
½ teaspoon thyme
½ teaspoon sage
Salt
Pepper

Preheat oven to 375°.

Combine zucchini, rice, wheat germ, 1 cup cheese, walnuts, mushrooms, green onions, eggs, oregano, garlic, and spices in large bowl. Mix until well blended. Pour into lightly greased 9″ × 5″ loaf pan. Sprinkle top with remaining cheese. Bake for 50 minutes, or until golden brown.

Makes 6 servings.

Pasta

ε❧ Besides the pasta dishes specifically mentioned in menus, here are a few pasta recipes that can be served almost any time of year as a main course or a side dish. Remember— pasta itself is not fattening. I repeat: Pasta is not fattening. It's all the oil, butter, and cheese we put on it that goes straight to the waist. So don't hesitate to eat pasta once in a while even if you're on a diet, but remember the key words SMALL PORTIONS!

Conchiglie (Shells) with Hot Sauce

2 cloves garlic, minced
2 tablespoons olive oil
8 cups (2 2-pound cans) Italian plum tomatoes
3 tablespoons chopped fresh basil
1 teaspoon crushed red pepper
1 pound conchiglie (pasta shells)
1 tablespoon butter
½ cup grated Romano cheese

Sauté garlic in oil until soft. Mash tomatoes in a bowl, then add to garlic oil with basil and red pepper, stirring well. Simmer, uncovered, stirring often until sauce begins to thicken.

Cook conchiglie in boiling water until al dente. Remove shells with a slotted spoon, and drain. Place in a warm bowl with butter and cheese, and toss. Add half of sauce, and mix well with pasta. Serve in warm bowls, each portion topped with a dollop of remaining sauce.

Serves 6.

Fettuccine Alfredo

1½ cups heavy cream
2 cups grated Parmesan cheese (about ½ pound)
½ cup butter
2 egg yolks
2 pounds fettuccine noodles
Parsley
Freshly ground pepper

Heat cream in a saucepan over very low heat. When cream begins to simmer, add cheese and stir almost constantly for about 10 minutes. Add butter, and continue to stir until sauce is smooth. Remove from heat. Using a whisk, beat about 1 cup sauce into egg yolks. Return yolk mixture to sauce, and whisk thoroughly.

Cook noodles in boiling water until they're slightly on the soft side of al dente, drain quickly in a colander, then transfer pasta to a large serving bowl. Pour cream sauce over noodles, and mix thoroughly. Garnish with chopped parsley and freshly ground pepper.

Serves 6 to 8.

Pasta Primavera

1 cup zucchini, sliced
1½ cups broccoli broken into flowerets
1½ cups snow peas
1 cup baby peas
6 stalks asparagus, sliced
1 pound spaghetti
16 cherry tomatoes, halved
4 cloves garlic, minced
Pepper
Olive oil
¼ cup Italian parsley, chopped

⅓ cup pine nuts
10 large mushrooms, sliced
½ cup butter
1 cup freshly grated Parmesan cheese, plus cheese for
  garnish
1 cup heavy cream
⅓ cup fresh basil
2 egg yolks, beaten

Blanch zucchini, broccoli, snow peas, peas, and asparagus in boiling salted water for 1–2 minutes. Vegetables should still be crisp.

Cook pasta until al dente. Drain.

While pasta cooks, sauté tomatoes in 1 tablespoon olive oil with half the garlic, pepper, and parsley. Set aside.

In another large pan, sauté pine nuts in 2 tablespoons oil until brown. Add remaining garlic, mushrooms, and all the blanched vegetables. Simmer a few minutes until hot.

In a pan large enough to hold pasta and vegetables, melt butter. Add cheese, cream, and basil. Stir to blend. Add egg yolks. Add pasta, and toss to coat with sauce. Add about ⅓ of vegetable mixture, and toss again.

Divide pasta among 6 soup plates, and top with remaining vegetables. Top with cherry tomatoes. Season to taste with pepper and additional Parmesan cheese.

Serves 6.

Pasta with Zucchini

3 small zucchini, unpeeled (2–3 inches long)
½ cup olive oil (reserve 1 tablespoon)
2 teaspoons thyme
Freshly ground pepper

Good commercial noodles or spaghetti
1 garlic clove, finely chopped
½ cup freshly grated Parmesan cheese

Wash and scrub zucchini and slice on the bias. Pat dry. Heat olive oil in a heavy-bottomed pan. Add zucchini, and sauté, stirring with a wooden spoon, over medium heat until zucchini are golden brown. Sprinkle with thyme and pepper.

Meanwhile, cook and drain pasta. Put zucchini on top of pasta, and sprinkle with 1 tablespoon olive oil, garlic, and cheese. Toss with 2 forks and serve.

Serves 6.

Spaghettini with Peas and Eggs

1 pound spaghettini
6 tablespoons grated Parmesan cheese
Pepper
2 cups shelled fresh peas, cooked al dente and drained
3 eggs, beaten

Cook spaghettini al dente. Drain, saving ⅓ cup of cooking water. Return spaghettini and water to pot. Over low heat, quickly blend in 2 tablespoons cheese, pepper, peas, and eggs. Toss well, and remove from heat before eggs set. Serve in large bowls with remaining cheese sprinkled on top.

Serves 6.

Spaghettini with Ricotta and Basil

2 cups Ricotta cheese
2 bunches fresh basil leaves
3 tablespoons Parmesan cheese

3 cloves garlic, chopped
2 tablespoons olive oil
1 pound spaghettini
1 Bermuda onion, chopped

In a blender or food processor, blend the Ricotta cheese, basil leaves, Parmesan cheese, garlic, and olive oil into a thick, slightly pasty consistency (add a bit more oil if the mixture feels too thick). Stir in chopped Bermuda onion.

Cook spaghettini al dente, and drain. Divide spaghettini among 6 bowls. Top each serving with a generous heaping of ricotta-basil sauce, then top with Marinated Tomatoes (recipe below).

Serves 6.

Marinated Tomatoes

4 fresh tomatoes, cut into quarters
½ cup oil
2 tablespoons vinegar
1 teaspoon oregano

Put chopped tomatoes into bowl containing other ingredients, and toss. Garnish hot Spaghettini with Ricotta and Basil with room temperature Marinated Tomatoes and liquid.

Side Dishes

Artichokes with Blueberry Rice

6 artichokes
1 lemon
1 cup uncooked white rice
2 cups vegetable bouillon or water
½ teaspoon rosemary, chopped fine
½ teaspoon dill leaves, chopped fine
¼ teaspoon powdered ginger
½ pound blueberries (or strawberries)
¼ pound butter
2 tablespoons parsley, chopped fine

Cut bottoms off artichokes, and trim spines from leaves with scissors. Place artichokes, root side down, in a large pot containing 3 or 4 inches of water plus the lemon, cut in eighths. Boil on very low heat for ½ hour.

Gently remove artichokes from pot. Carefully remove each "choke," the thistle covering of the artichoke heart, and gently spread leaves to make a commodious well for the stuffing. Cool.

In a large pot, boil rice, bouillon or water, rosemary, dill, and ginger until water is almost completely absorbed, 10–15 minutes. Add washed blueberries (or strawberries), and cook 5 minutes. Stir gently until a purple blueberry color is uniform.

Stuff artichokes with "royal rice" mixture, spooning it into the well.

Melt butter and chopped parsley over low heat, about 2 minutes.

Serve cool artichokes with parsleyed butter in separate dish for dipping artichoke leaves.

Serves 6.

Lemon Asparagus

6 hard-boiled eggs, mashed
1½ cups butter, melted
Salt
Freshly ground pepper
3 tablespoons fresh lemon juice
3 tablespoons minced parsley
4 pounds asparagus, trimmed and peeled

Combine mashed eggs, butter, salt, and pepper in a small saucepan. Cook over low heat long enough to heat through. Remove from heat and stir in lemon juice and parsley; keep hot while asparagus is cooking. Turn into a sauceboat and serve as soon as asparagus is ready.

Cook asparagus. Drain on a cloth napkin; cover with the overlapping part of the napkin to absorb any moisture remaining in asparagus.

Serves 6.

Asparagus Maltaise

Maltaise Sauce
2 egg yolks
2 tablespoons plain yogurt
1 tablespoon fresh lemon juice
1 tablespoon dry sherry
½ cup vegetable oil

1 teaspoon finely grated orange peel
⅛ teaspoon sea salt or ¼ teaspoon coarse salt
Ground red pepper

24 to 36 medium-size fresh asparagus spears, well trimmed
  and steamed crisp-tender

Combine egg yolks, yogurt, lemon juice, and sherry in a small
bowl, and beat with a small whisk. Set bowl in medium skillet
half filled with hot water. Beat mixture over low heat until thick.
Whisking constantly, gradually add oil in a slow, steady stream.
Stir in orange peel, salt, and pepper.

Transfer sauce to a small bowl set in the center of a serving
platter, and surround with asparagus spears.

Serves 6.

Note: Maltaise Sauce can be prepared up to 6 hours ahead. Let
stand at room temperature or leave in warm-water bath.

Beets and Sweet Potato Pie

2 bunches beets and tops (6 medium beets)
1 large sweet potato
½ pound carrots
1 medium white onion
1 clove garlic, chopped
2 tablespoons butter
¼ teaspoon curry powder
¼ teaspoon cinnamon
2 tablespoons grated orange rind (reserve a bit for garnish)
½ cup orange juice
6 ounces cranberries
2 tablespoons honey
½ cup heavy cream
1 9-inch pie plate and pastry
1 cake tofu

Preheat oven to 350°.

Remove tops from beets, wash thoroughly to remove all sand, and steam until slightly wilted. Trim beets and potato and boil until just tender. Remove from heat, reserving 1 cup of cooking liquid, and slice beets and potato into round, fairly thin slices. Sauté carrots, onion, and garlic in butter until all are just tender, then add curry powder, cinnamon, and orange rind, and simmer for 5 minutes. In a blender, purée reserved beet-and-potato liquid, orange juice, cranberries, honey, and cream.

Cover bottom of piecrust with a layer of beet greens. Cut tofu into thin slices and layer it on beet greens; then add a layer of beets, a layer of carrot mixture, a layer of potato slices, and so on until pie is well packed and slightly rounded. Pour half the sauce on top, cover with beet greens, and bake for 30 minutes.

Remove from oven, pour remaining sauce over pie, and garnish with orange rind.

Serves 6 as a side dish.

Sesame Broccoli

1 large bunch broccoli, broken into flowerets, stems peeled
½ cup sesame seed, toasted
¼ cup sake
1½ tablespoons soy sauce
2 teaspoons sesame oil
2 teaspoons honey

Cook broccoli in boiling salted water until crisp-tender. Drain thoroughly. Let cool to room temperature.

Combine remaining ingredients in large bowl. Shortly before serving, add broccoli and toss to mix well.

Serves 6.

Broccoli with Sauce Piquante

2 tablespoons olive oil
4 shallots, chopped
2 tablespoons red wine vinegar
⅓ cup dry white wine
Freshly ground pepper
3 tomatoes, peeled and chopped, or 1 16-ounce can
1 garlic clove, crushed
Salt
4 gherkins, chopped
⅓ cup capers
1 pound broccoli

Trim broccoli and steam until just tender. Heat oil in a heavy-bottomed pan and add shallots, vinegar, wine, and pepper. Boil for 5 minutes, then add chopped tomatoes, garlic, and salt. Cook over low heat for 15 minutes. Remove from heat and stir in gherkins and capers. Pour over broccoli and serve.

Serves 6.

Brussels Sprouts with Garlic and Parmesan

1 pound fresh Brussels sprouts
¼ cup water
2 tablespoons butter (¼ stick)
1 garlic clove, minced
Salt
Freshly ground pepper
¼ cup freshly grated Parmesan cheese

Discard any dry outside leaves from sprouts. Trim stems. Using small, sharp knife, cut a shallow x in bottom of each stem. Combine sprouts and water in a shallow 1-quart baking dish. Cover and cook on high 7 minutes. Let rest, covered, 3–4 minutes.

Meanwhile, combine butter and garlic in small glass measuring cup and cook on high 1–2 minutes. Drain water from sprouts. Add butter mixture, salt, and pepper, and toss lightly to coat. Add cheese and toss again. Serve hot.

Serves 6 to 8.

Spiced Cabbage

1 large cabbage
2 onions, chopped
2 apples, peeled, cored, and cut into ½-inch cubes
2 tablespoons butter
½ teaspoon cinnamon
Salt
Pepper

Shred or chop cabbage, and boil in a covered saucepan for 3 minutes, then drain and set aside.

Fry onions and apples in butter until soft. Sprinkle with cinnamon, add cabbage, and toss over low heat for 3 minutes. Season to taste with salt and pepper, and serve.

Serves 6.

Sweet and Sour Carrots

10 carrots
1½ cups water
¾ teaspoon salt
2 tablespoons butter
2 teaspoons flour
1 tablespoon sugar
1 tablespoon vinegar

Wash, scrape, and thinly slice carrots. Combine carrots in a saucepan with water and salt; bring to a boil and cook over low heat for 10 minutes. Drain, reserving 1 cup liquid.

Melt butter in a saucepan; blend in flour. Add reserved liquid, stirring steadily to the boiling point. Mix in sugar, vinegar, and carrots. Cook over low heat for 5 minutes.

Serves 4 to 6.

Cauliflower with Vinegar and Tomatoes

1 large head cauliflower, cut into flowerets
6 tablespoons olive oil
1 cup chopped onion
3 tablespoons wine vinegar
1 cup chopped tomato
1 tablespoon dried sweet basil
Freshly ground pepper

Blanch cauliflower flowerets in boiling water. Remove cauliflower and drain. Place cauliflower and olive oil in a skillet, and cook, uncovered, over moderate heat until edges of cauliflower begin to brown. Add onion. When onion wilts, add vinegar, cover, and continue to cook over low heat for 3–4 minutes. Add tomato, basil, and pepper to taste. Cover and simmer until cauliflower is just al dente.

Serves 6.

Celery Root Purée

3 quarts water
2 tablespoons salt
2½ pounds celery root, peeled and cut into 3-inch pieces

2 large potatoes (1 pound total), peeled and cut into 3-inch
 pieces
¼ cup (½ stick) unsalted butter (room temperature), cut
 into 2 pieces
¼ cup (4 tablespoons) parsley leaves, minced (use steel
 knife)
½ teaspoon freshly grated nutmeg
Freshly ground pepper

Preheat oven to 300°.

Generously butter 5-cup baking dish, preferably glass. Bring
water to boil with salt in large saucepan. Add celery root and
potatoes, and boil until soft, about 15–20 minutes. drain well.
Return to saucepan and place over low heat, shaking constantly, until moisture has evaporated and vegetables are dry.

Transfer vegetables to a work bowl. Add butter and purée. Add
3 tablespoons parsley, nutmeg, and pepper, and blend well.
Spoon into prepared dish, smoothing top with spatula. Cover
with foil. (Can be prepared ahead to this point and refrigerated.
Bring purée to room temperature before baking.) Bake, covered, until heated through, about 30 minutes. Top with remaining parsley.

Serves 8.

Corn Soufflé

3 tablespoons all-purpose flour
1 cup milk
⅓ teaspoon prepared mustard
⅛ teaspoon chili powder
½ teaspoon salt
1 cup grated medium-sharp Cheddar cheese
1½ cups fresh corn kernels (from 3 ears)
4 eggs, separated
⅛ teaspoon baking powder

Preheat oven to 350°.

Combine small amount of flour with milk. Then add remaining flour to make a paste. Add mustard, chili powder, and salt. Heat mixture in a heavy saucepan over medium heat, and add cheese. Cut raw corn kernels from ears and scrape corn milk from cobs with a knife. Add to sauce mixture. Separate eggs. Put egg yolks into a 1-quart mixing bowl, and beat lightly. Add small amount of hot corn mixture to yolks, then mix in remainder. In another bowl, beat egg whites with baking powder until whites form soft peaks. Fold into corn mixture. Place an ungreased 1½-quart casserole in a pan of warm water and pour mixture into casserole. Run the tip of a knife around mixture about 1 inch from edge. Place in hot oven and bake for 55 minutes. Soufflé is ready to serve when the point of a knife inserted in the center comes out clean.

Serves 6.

Pepper-Corn Bake

2 cups sweet corn kernels
1 cup chopped jalapeño pepper
1 cup chopped red pepper
½ cup chopped onion
2 tablespoons chopped parsley
1 tablespoon butter, melted
¾ cup cornmeal
¼ cup cream
2 eggs, beaten
Salt

Preheat oven to 350°.

Combine all ingredients in a bowl. Pour into a buttered loaf pan or cake tin that has been sprinkled with cornmeal. Bake until set, about 30 minutes. Serve warm.

Serves 6.

Szechwan Eggplant

2 medium eggplants (about 1 pound each)
Salad oil
1¾ cups water
2 tablespoons soy sauce
1 tablespoon sugar
1 tablespoon cornstarch
1 tablespoon minced, peeled gingerroot, or 1¼ teaspoons
    ground ginger
1 teaspoon hot pepper sauce
¼ teaspoon salt
1 green onion, finely chopped

About 1 hour before serving, cut eggplants lengthwise into ½-inch-thick slices; cut each slice lengthwise in half. In 12-inch skillet over medium-high heat, in ¼ cup hot salad oil, cook eggplant, a few slices at a time, until browned on both sides. Remove browned slices to paper towel to drain, adding more oil to skillet if needed.

In same skillet, mix water and remaining ingredients. Cook over medium heat, stirring constantly, until mixture boils and thickens slightly. Return eggplant to skillet; heat through.

Makes 8 accompaniment servings.

Sautéed Fennel

Fennel is a delicious, much overlooked vegetable, used mostly in Italian cooking.

4 or 5 medium-size heads of fennel
½ cup olive oil
3 garlic cloves
Salt
Pepper
½ cup dry white wine

Cut "fingers" with their green tops flush off the fennel heads. Trim base and remove tough outer leaves. Cut large fennel heads lengthwise into 8 pieces, or cut small or medium-size fennel into quarters. Place in a saucepan and barely cover with boiling salted water. Cook, covered, for 3–5 minutes; the fennel should be barely tender. Drain fennel.

Heat olive oil in a large frying pan. Cook garlic cloves in oil until brown. Discard garlic. Add fennel, sprinkle lightly with salt and freshly ground pepper, and add wine. Reduce heat to low, cover pan, and cook for 5–10 minutes. Serve hot.

Serves 6.

Green Beans with Basil

A simple side dish, green beans are at their absolute sweetest and most delicate in spring.

Savory
1½ pounds green beans
Rosemary
¼ pound sweet butter
1 bunch fresh basil
1 lemon
Parsley

In a large saucepan, bring 2 cups water to a boil, and drop in a few sprigs (or 1 teaspoon dried) savory. Simmer, covered, for as long as it takes to wash and cut tops and tails off the beans. Remove savory and drop in beans. Mix 1 teaspoon dried rosemary into beans, and keep water boiling so that beans are partly steamed as water boils down. Cook for about 15 minutes.

Soften 4 tablespoons butter in a bowl, chop up basil, and combine with softened butter and juice of the lemon. Put aside.

After beans have cooked for 15 minutes, stir in 2 tablespoons plain butter and begin tasting for perfect doneness. (Beans should be a little crisp.) Pour off remaining liquid, and put beans back on low heat to dry out.

Pile beans on a hot platter, dot with basil butter, and sprinkle with chopped parsley.

Serves 6.

Kasha

1 cup kasha (buckwheat groats)
1 egg, lightly beaten
1 tablespoon butter
2 cups water

Combine egg and kasha until kasha grains are all coated. Melt butter in a saucepan and add kasha. Cook, stirring frequently, until grains are just dry and not browned. Add water to cover kasha, cover pan, bring to a boil, and let simmer until liquid is absorbed.

Serves 6.

Leeks with Caper Sauce

12 small leeks
5 large lettuce leaves
½ cup finely chopped gherkin pickles
1 tablespoon finely chopped capers
½ cup olive oil
3 tablespoons white wine vinegar

Prepare leeks by trimming off roots and green leaves. Cut in half lengthwise. Wash thoroughly to remove sand. Place leeks in vegetable steamer with 1 inch salted water. Cover and steam for 20 minutes or until fork tender. Drain well. Transfer to a shallow serving dish lined with lettuce. Set aside.

In a small bowl combine pickles, capers, oil, and vinegar; beat well with a wire whisk. Pour over leeks and let stand for at least 30 minutes before serving.

Serves 6 as side dish or appetizer.

Mee Siam

A long-established favorite in Singapore and Malaysia, these Thai-style noodles make a terrific snack or an elegant side dish.

1 pound rice vermicelli
Oil
2 cakes hard tofu
1 pound bean sprouts
1 cup coarse chives (kuchai), garlic cloves, or spring onions, cut in 1-inch lengths
3 hard-boiled eggs, peeled and quartered lengthwise
6 Chinese limes, halved, or 2 large limes or lemons, cut in wedges

Spice Paste:
10–15 dried red chilies, soaked in hot water until soft
12–15 shallots or 2 medium red onions
1 stalk lemon grass or piece of thin lemon peel
3 tablespoons oil
2 heaping tablespoons salted soybeans, lightly crushed
1 teaspoon salt
1 tablespoon sugar

Gravy
4 cups thin coconut milk
2 tablespoons dried tamarind pulp
1 cup warm water

Prepare Spice Paste first. Blend chilies, shallots, and lemon grass in a food processor until fine, adding a little oil to keep blades turning. Heat oil in a wok and gently fry Spice Paste for

3–4 minutes, stirring constantly. Sprinkle in salt, sugar, and crushed soybeans, and continue cooking for another minute. Remove half the mixture and use for Gravy. Set aside wok with remaining spice paste.

To make Gravy, put reserved Spice Paste into a deep saucepan and add coconut milk. Bring to a boil, stirring constantly to prevent curdling. Soak tamarind in warm water for 10 minutes, then strain through a sieve to obtain juice. Add tamarind juice to coconut milk, simmer a couple of minutes, and set aside.

Soak rice vermicelli in hot water for 5 minutes, then drain and set aside. Heat oil in a pan and deep fry tofu until golden brown on both sides. Drain, cool, then slice coarsely. Have all other ingredients prepared and placed on a plate for easy assembly.

Just before serving, heat Spice Paste remaining in wok. Add bean sprouts and cook over high heat, stirring constantly, for 1 minute. Add half the chives, stir, then add drained vermicelli, a handful at a time, stirring constantly to mix well with other ingredients and heat through. Place in a large serving dish, and scatter remaining chives on top. Arrange eggs, tofu, and limes around the edge. Serve Gravy separately in a deep bowl. Each diner puts noodles into his or her bowl, adds Gravy and squeezes plenty of lime juice on top. If you like really hot food, serve additional freshly ground red chilies.

Serves 6.

Note: Miss Page and I discovered that in Singapore they really like their food *hot*! In eating Satay at the Rendezvous, it didn't take us long to adopt the native custom of shoveling—quite literally—a huge spoonful of rice into your mouth after every spoonful of Satay-covered whatever.

Creamed Onions

18 small white onions
3 tablespoons butter
3 tablespoons flour

1½ cups milk
⅓ cup chopped parsley
¼ teaspoon paprika

Cook onions in their skins until tender, 20 minutes or longer. Drain and peel. In a saucepan, melt butter, add flour, and stir with a whisk until blended. Meanwhile, bring milk to a boil, and add all at once to butter-flour mixture, whisking vigorously until sauce is smooth and thickened. Add sauce to onions and reheat. Sprinkle with parsley and paprika.

Serves 6.

Bombay Rice-Stuffed Onions

½ cup golden raisins
2 tablespoons bourbon
12 medium onions
2 tablespoons butter or margarine
1 cup raw rice
2½ cups water
1 teaspoon salt
1 cup shredded carrots
1 teaspoon grated orange peel
½ teaspoon mace
12 pecan halves
Orange Glaze (see page 148)

Soak raisins in bourbon at least 30 minutes.

Cook onions in boiling salted water just until tender, about 10 or 12 minutes. Drain and cool slightly. Cut slice from top of each onion and remove all but ¾ inch of shell. Remove a small slice from the bottom so onion will stand level.

Preheat oven to 350°.

Sauté onion pulp in butter in 10-inch skillet until golden. Add rice. Cook and stir over low heat until rice is golden, about 3 minutes. Add water and salt. Bring to boil. Cover tightly and simmer 20 minutes. Remove from heat.

Stir in raisins, carrots, orange peel, and mace. Place onion shells in buttered baking dish. Mound about ½ cup rice mixture in each onion cup, and top with pecan halves. Spoon Orange Glaze over each onion. Bake, uncovered, until hot, about 10–15 minutes.

Serves 6.

Orange Glaze

1 cup orange juice
3 tablespoons butter, softened
1 tablespoon flour
2 tablespoons brown sugar

Heat orange juice in small saucepan. Combine butter and flour. Stir into orange juice. Add brown sugar. Bring to boil, stirring constantly. Reduce heat and cook, stirring until slightly thickened.

Braised Parsnips

Proving that you *can* teach an old dog new tricks, two years ago I wouldn't eat parsnips. Now I will, and so will you. Especially done this way.

3 tablespoons butter
2 pounds parsnips, peeled and cut into thin julienne strips
1 tablespoon grated onion
¼ teaspoon freshly ground pepper

¼ teaspoon sugar
6 large outer romaine lettuce leaves
4 tablespoons parsley, minced

Heat butter in a saucepan. Add parsnips, onion, pepper, and sugar. Mix gently with a wooden fork. Wash lettuce leaves and cover the parsnips with lettuce. Simmer, covered, over low heat for 10–15 minutes or until parsnips are tender. Stir occasionally to prevent sticking. Garnish with minced parsley before serving with lettuce leaves, which will have wilted in cooking.

Serves 6.

Peas with Cream and Mint

2 tablespoons butter
4 pounds peas (unshelled weight), shelled (about 4 cups)
⅓ cup water
Salt
2 sprigs fresh mint or 1 teaspoon dried mint
⅛ teaspoon saffron or ground turmeric
½ cup heavy cream

Heat butter in a heavy saucepan. Add peas, water, salt, and mint. Simmer, covered, over low heat for about 10 minutes or until tender. If peas look soupy, cook uncovered to allow pan liquid to evaporate. Remove mint from cooked peas. While peas are cooking, stir saffron or turmeric into cream. Whip just a little and fold into cooked peas. Serve immediately.

Serves 6.

Hungarian Sour Potatoes

2½ pounds tiny new potatoes
2 tablespoons butter or oil
2 tablespoons flour

2 tablespoons chopped onion
1 teaspoon caraway seeds (optional)
1 tablespoon dry white wine or lemon juice
¼ teaspoon sugar
2 teaspoons sour cream
Salt
Pepper

Cook potatoes, covered, in boiling, salted water to cover until tender (about 20–30 minutes). Drain but reserve cooking liquid. Shake potatoes in their saucepan over low heat until they are quite dry. (Steam will cease to appear.)

Heat butter or oil in a skillet. Add flour and mix until a brown paste is formed. Add onion and cook until soft. Add 1 cup reserved liquid from potatoes. If there is not enough liquid, add water to make 1 cup, and stir until thickened. Add potatoes and caraway. Simmer for a few minutes. Add wine or juice, sugar, sour cream, and seasonings, and bring to a boil. Serve immediately.

Serves 6.

Lemon Potatoes

2 pounds small new potatoes or other potatoes
Boiling salted water
4 tablespoons olive oil
2 tablespoons fresh lemon juice
Grated rind of ½ lemon
Salt
Freshly ground pepper
1 teaspoon dried oregano (optional)

If potatoes are small and new, scrub but do not peel them. Or peel potatoes and cut into 2-inch pieces. Cook potatoes in plenty of boiling water until barely tender. Drain and return to saucepan. Over moderate heat, shake saucepan containing potatoes to dry them out completely. Put into a heated serving dish and keep warm.

While potatoes are cooking, combine remaining ingredients and beat until creamy. Pour over potatoes, toss with two forks, and serve dish warm, lukewarm, or chilled.

Serves 4 to 6.

Rice with Tomatoes, Chilies, and Coconut

1 cup fresh coconut, peeled and chopped
1½ cups hot water
2 tablespoons olive oil
½ cup finely chopped onion
1 small bell pepper, finely chopped
1 cup uncooked rice
2 tomatoes, peeled and finely chopped
1 teaspoon salt
2 teaspoons finely minced fresh, hot chilies

In a blender combine coconut and hot water; blend until smooth. Heat the oil in a heavy skillet. Add onion and bell pepper, and cook, stirring frequently, until they are soft but not brown. Add rice, and stir for a few minutes until grains are evenly coated. Stir in coconut liquid, tomatoes, and salt, and bring to a simmer over moderate heat. Cover pan tightly, reduce heat to its lowest point, and simmer for about 20 minutes or until all liquid has been absorbed. Remove pan from heat, stir in chilies, and taste for seasoning. Cover again and let rice rest at room temperature for about 10 minutes before serving. When ready, fluff rice gently with a fork and place in heated bowl.

Serves 4.

Glazed Squash-Pecan

5 pounds Hubbard or banana squash, cut in large pieces
3 tablespoons butter
3 tablespoons brown sugar

⅓ cup light raisins
¼ teaspoon ground nutmeg
⅛ teaspoon pepper
1 tablespoon light corn syrup
2 tablespoons chopped pecans

Preheat oven to 400°.

Place squash, cut side down, in 15″ × 10″ × 1″ baking pan. Bake until tender, 65 to 75 minutes. Scoop out pulp into mixer bowl. Whip pulp with 2 tablespoons butter and 2 tablespoons brown sugar. Turn mixture into large kettle or Dutch oven. Cook, uncovered, stirring occasionally, over medium heat until mixture begins to thicken, 5–10 minutes. Stir in raisins, nutmeg, and pepper. Cook 5 minutes more, stirring frequently. Turn into serving dish.

In small saucepan, heat remaining butter, brown sugar, and corn syrup until sugar is dissolved. Stir in pecans. Drizzle over squash.

Makes 8 servings.

Summer Squash Soufflé

3 cups cooked summer squash
4 tablespoons butter
2 tablespoons brown sugar
½ teaspoon grated orange rind
¼ teaspoon nutmeg
½ teaspoon salt
Pepper
4 egg yolks
4 egg whites

Reheat oven to 375°.

Mash squash, and mix and beat with butter, brown sugar, orange rind, nutmeg, salt, and pepper until thoroughly blended. Add egg yolks and beat well. Beat egg whites until stiff, then fold into squash mixture. Place squash in a buttered soufflé dish. Bake for 45–60 minutes.

Serves 6 to 8.

Tangerine-Sweet Potato Bake

This recipe makes excellent use of the highly underrated tangerine.

6 medium sweet potatoes, peeled
2 tablespoons butter
3 tablespoons brown sugar
3 tablespoons light rum
4 tangerines, peeled
2 tablespoons walnuts or toasted almonds

Preheat oven to 350°.

Boil sweet potatoes until soft, about 30 minutes, and mash. Add butter, brown sugar, and rum, and whip. Split 2 peeled tangerines in half, remove seeds, and fold fruit into mixture. Put mixture into a casserole dish. Split the remaining 2 tangerines into sections, remove pits, and place sections on top of casserole. Sprinkle with walnuts or toasted almonds. Bake at 350° for 25–30 minutes.

Serves 6 to 8.

Vegetables with Ginger

8 small boiling potatoes
3 large carrots, peeled, cut lengthwise into quarters and
   then crosswise in 2-inch lengths
½ pound fresh green beans, cut in 2-inch lengths

4 tablespoons vegetable oil
2 onions, quartered and cut in ½-inch slices
1 large green pepper, cut in strips
2 whole fresh chilies, finely chopped
1 tablespoon finely chopped garlic
2 tablespoons finely chopped fresh gingerroot
½ teaspoon white pepper
6 green onions, cut in 2-inch lengths, green tops included

Peel potatoes; then, with a small, sharp knife, cut out narrow V-shaped wedges ¼-inch deep at ½-inch intervals all around the length of the potatoes. In a large kettle, boil lightly salted water and drop in potatoes, carrots, and beans. Let vegetables boil briskly, uncovered, for 5 minutes. Drain in a colander and run cold water over them to stop cooking.

In a heavy, large casserole, heat oil until hot. Add onions, green pepper, and chilies, and cook, stirring frequently, for about 5 minutes or until vegetables are soft but not brown. Add garlic, ginger, and pepper, and stir for a few minutes. Add potatoes, carrots, beans, and green onions to casserole. Stir until vegetables are coated with oil mixture. Reduce heat to low, and cook for about 10 minutes or until vegetables are tender but still somewhat crisp. Serve immediately.

Serves 4.

Gado-Gado (Cooked Vegetables with Peanut Sauce)

1 cup fresh green beans, sliced into 1-inch pieces
1 cup carrots, sliced into ¼-inch pieces
1 cup sliced cabbage
1 cup cauliflower flowerets
¼ pound bean sprouts (fresh, or rinsed and drained canned)
1 cucumber, sliced
2 large boiling potatoes, boiled and sliced
Kacang Saus (recipe below)

Blanch beans, carrots, cabbage, and cauliflower separately in lightly salted water for 3 minutes each. Drain vegetables and arrange on platter. Top with bean sprouts and surround with cucumber and potato slices. Serve from platter, topping each plate with Kacang Saus.

Serves 6.

Kacang Saus (Peanut Sauce)

1½ cups salted Spanish peanuts with skins (not dry-roasted) or peanut butter
1 tablespoon peanut oil
¼ cup chopped onion
4 garlic cloves, minced
1½ cups coconut milk or canned coconut cream
1½–2 teaspoons sambal oelek (crushed chili paste), crushed red pepper, or chili powder
1 teaspoon ground ginger
¼ teaspoon ground cumin
3 tablespoons fresh lemon juice
4–5 tablespoons soy sauce

Place peanuts in food processor or blender, and mix to paste or butter, stopping to scrape down sides as necessary.

Heat oil in small saucepan. Add onion and garlic, and sauté about 1 minute. Stirring constantly, add coconut milk, sambal oelek, ginger, cumin, lemon juice, and soy sauce, and bring to a boil. Whisk in peanut butter and cook, stirring constantly, until sauce is thickened, about 3–5 minutes.

Makes about 2 cups.

Dressings and Sauces

Green Goddess Dressing

2 tablespoons finely chopped fresh chives or 1 tablespoon
   dried chives
1 clove garlic, minced
5 tablespoons chopped fresh parsley
1 tablespoon chopped scallions
2 cups sour cream
1 cup mayonnaise (see page 158)
1 tablespoon lemon juice
3 tablespoons tarragon vinegar
Pepper

Place chives, garlic, parsley, and scallions in a mixing bowl.
Add sour cream and mayonnaise, and stir. Season with lemon
juice and vinegar. Stir, adding pepper to taste. Cover and chill.
Stir again before serving.

Makes 3 cups.

Creamy Herb Tofu Dressing

3 tablespoons lemon juice
1 tablespoon tamari or soy sauce
1 tablespoon safflower oil
3 tablespoons water
1 clove garlic, minced
½ teaspoon powdered ginger
¼ teaspoon basil
¼ teaspoon marjoram

¼ teaspoon celery seed
Pinch cayenne pepper
¼ cup chopped fresh parsley
1 cup tofu, mashed

Combine all ingredients except tofu in a blender or food processor. With blender running, add mashed tofu, a little at a time, until dressing is very smooth. (If necessary, add 2–3 teaspoons water to obtain a thick and creamy consistency.)

Makes about 1 cup.

Lemon-Mustard Dressing

¾ cup dry white wine, preferably Chablis
2 tablespoons dry mustard
8 egg yolks
2 cups vegetable oil
3 tablespoons fresh lemon juice
1 tablespoon chopped fresh chives or parsley
1 teaspoon sugar

Combine wine with mustard in large mixing bowl, and let stand ½ hour. Add egg yolks, and mix well with whisk. Add oil very slowly, beating constantly. When dressing is thick, blend in remaining ingredients. Serve chilled.

Makes 1 quart.

Mayonnaise

There's nothing wrong with store-bought mayonnaise. But if you're a purist this homemade version is delicious.

2 egg yolks
¼ teaspoon salt (optional)
2 teaspoons Dijon mustard
3 teaspoons lemon juice
1 cup olive oil or salad oil

Place all ingredients, except oil, in a food processor or blender, and blend for about 10 minutes, or until combined. Add oil slowly in a steady stream. Mixture will begin to thicken; because this recipe calls for 2 egg yolks, mayonnaise will thicken quickly.

Makes approximately 1½ cups.

Roquefort-Sour Cream Dressing

2 tablespoons cider vinegar
½ teaspoon dry mustard
1 teaspoon chopped shallots
1 cup sour cream
2 ounces Roquefort or blue cheese
Pepper

Combine vinegar, mustard, and shallots, and add sour cream, stirring to blend well. Crumble cheese into mixture, stir again, and season to taste with pepper. Chill before serving.

Makes about 1½ cups.

Vinaigrette Dressing

4 tablespoons wine vinegar
16 tablespoons olive oil
½ teaspoon dry mustard
Pinch each of oregano, basil, tarragon, and thyme

Combine vinegar and oil in a bowl, and beat with a whisk until mixture thickens slightly. Add remaining ingredients, and whisk again briskly for about 10 seconds. Chill; whisk again before serving.

Makes 1 cup.

Note: The ratio for more dressing: 1 tablespoon vinegar to 4 tablespoons oil.

Cranapple Relish

This excellent recipe is from *The Food Processor Cookbook* by my friend Carmel Berman Rheingold. It's a wonderful accompaniment for any number of foods, especially Corn Fritters (recipe on page 109).

1 cup shelled walnuts
1 cup sugar (or to taste)
1 cup fresh, uncooked cranberries
2 apples, peeled, cored, and cut into quarters
½ cup orange juice

Place metal blade in food processor. Add all ingredients to processor. Pulse machine on and off for approximately 10 seconds, or until ingredients are coarsely chopped. Spoon relish into bowl and cover. Chill overnight.

Makes 4 cups.

Note: This can be made in a blender as well.

Béchamel Sauce

3 tablespoons butter
½ medium onion, minced
3 tablespoons flour
2½ cups hot milk
Several peppercorns
Large pinch of whole thyme
1 small bay leaf
Salt to taste
Dash of nutmeg

Melt butter either in top of a large double boiler or in a heavy-bottomed, enameled medium saucepan. Add minced onion, and cook over low heat, stirring frequently, until onion is soft but not brown. Stir in flour, and continue cooking roux for a few minutes more, stirring often. Add hot milk, beating it in with a whisk until sauce is perfectly smooth and beginning to thicken. Add a few peppercorns, a good pinch of whole thyme, a tiny bay leaf, a little salt, and a little nutmeg. Cook sauce over very gentle heat, stirring often, for at least 10–15 minutes or for as long as 1 hour. The longer the cooking time, the thicker and stronger flavored the sauce.

Strain sauce through a sieve, and dot with small shavings of butter, which will melt and keep a skin from forming on top.

Makes 2½–3 cups.

Mornay Sauce

4 tablespoons grated Swiss cheese
3 tablespoons grated Parmesan cheese
Hot Béchamel Sauce
Dash of cayenne pepper (optional)

Add grated cheeses to hot Béchamel Sauce. Beat with a whisk until cheeses have melted and sauce is perfectly smooth. Add cayenne pepper if desired.

Makes about 3 cups.

Walnut Sauce

½ cup chopped walnuts
1 garlic clove, crushed
3 tablespoons olive oil
3 tablespoons warm water

Mash walnuts and garlic (preferably with a pestle in a mortar) until they are of smooth texture. Add oil, a little at a time, stirring constantly. Add warm water. The result should be a smooth sauce. Serve with practically any vegetable side dish.

Serves 6.

Bread, Muffins, and Pie Pastry

ABOUT BREAD

These bread recipes have come to me not only from Miss Page, but from many close and trusted friends—loaves still warm from the oven as testament to their being homemade.

I, personally, don't bake bread, basically because years ago I baked a beautiful sourdough loaf that dropped out of my hands and broke my foot. Besides, I'm not particularly fond of serving bread with dinner (unless it's strictly a hot soup or huge salad meal), as I'd rather my guests not fill up before the real food comes.

However, nearly everyone I know who bakes bread—and that includes nearly everyone I know—swears it's fun and rewarding, so here are some of their recipes, which I promise you'll enjoy.

Meantime, I'll continue to get "my loaf to keep me warm" at my neighborhood bakery.

Black Bread

1 tablespoon active dry yeast
1½ cups warm water
1 cup gluten flour
2 cups whole-wheat flour
1 cup wheat bran
1 cup dark rye flour
1 cup wheat germ
½ cup rolled oats

I personally don't bake bread.

1 cup warm water
½ cup blackstrap molasses
4 teaspoons salt
½–1 cup additional whole-wheat flour
Rolled oats

Dissolve yeast in warm water in a large, shallow bowl. Stir in gluten and whole-wheat flours, and knead vigorously until you have a rubbery ball of dough. Spread this dough over bottom and slightly up sides of bowl. Sprinkle remaining ingredients, except additional whole-wheat flour and rolled oats, over dough. Using a potato masher, mix ingredients until they are well distributed. Knead dough until it is the same color and texture throughout; then knead in additional whole-wheat flour until dough is no longer sticky.

Let dough rise in a warm place until doubled in bulk, at least 1 hour. Punch down, and shape into 2 loaves. Roll loaves in rolled oats, place side by side on a greased cookie sheet, and let bread rise again for about 45 minutes.

Preheat oven to 350°. Bake for 45 minutes or longer.

Makes 2 loaves.

Bran Muffins

Miss Page made these muffins, and they are absolutely scrumptious. I actually found myself eating them as if they were bonbons—so if you're dieting, beware.

2 cups whole-wheat flour
1½ cups pure bran
2 tablespoons brown sugar
1 teaspoon salt
1¼ teaspoons baking soda
2 cups buttermilk
1 egg
½ cup dark molasses
2 tablespoons butter, melted

Preheat oven to 350°.

Combine flour, bran, brown sugar, salt, and soda, and mix well. Combine buttermilk, egg, molasses, and butter. Add all at once to dry ingredients, and stir just to moisten flour mixture. Spoon into well-greased muffin cups, filling two-thirds full. Bake 20–25 minutes.

Makes 24 muffins.

Corn Bread

2 cups cornmeal
½ cup wheat germ
1 teaspoon salt
½ teaspoon baking soda
1 teaspoon baking powder
1 tablespoon brown sugar
1 large egg, beaten
1 tablespoon oil
2 cups buttermilk
Butter for pan

Preheat oven to 425°.

In a large bowl, stir together dry ingredients. In another bowl, mix wet ingredients. Combine the two just until they are well mixed. Turn into a well-greased 8″ × 8″ baking pan. Bake for 20–25 minutes.

Makes 12 squares.

Sour Cream Corn Muffins

1¼ cups cornmeal
¾ cup whole-wheat flour
3 teaspoons baking powder
½ teaspoon salt

1 egg
¾ cup milk
2 tablespoons honey
½ cup sour cream
¾ cup raisins

Preheat oven to 400°.

Mix cornmeal, flour, baking powder, and salt in a bowl. Beat egg, and combine with milk and honey. Add to cornmeal mixture, and mix well. Stir in sour cream, then raisins. Turn batter into well-greased or paper-lined muffin cups, and bake for 15–20 minutes.

Makes 12 muffins.

Mustard Beer Bread

This recipe is from *The Mustard Cookbook* by Sally and Martin Stone (Avon). The fact that they are friends and neighbors has not influenced my decision to include it here. The fact that they are friends and neighbors who have brought me loaves of this bread and from whom I want more, more, more—that's what influenced my decision.

2 packages active dry yeast
½ cup lukewarm water
1 tablespoon sugar
½ cup butter
1 cup beer
2 teaspoons salt
1 cup Dijon mustard
¼ cup plus 2 teaspoons white mustard seeds
6 cups all-purpose flour
1 egg white beaten with 1 tablespoon cold water

Dissolve yeast in lukewarm water. Add sugar, and set aside.

Melt butter in a saucepan, and stir in beer, salt, mustard, and ¼ cup mustard seeds. Place mixture in bowl of an electric mixer fitted with a dough hook. Add yeast mixture. On low speed, add flour 1 cup at a time. Mix until dough clings to hook and leaves side of bowl. Continue to knead on low speed for about 10 minutes, until dough is smooth and elastic. (To mix by hand, place butter mixture and yeast mixture in a large bowl. Add flour, 1 cup at a time, and mix with a wooden spoon until a dough is formed. Turn out onto a lightly floured surface, and knead for about 10 minutes until dough is smooth and elastic.)

Place dough in a warm, oiled bowl. Oil top of dough. Cover bowl with a clean, dry towel, and place in a warm spot (80°–85°) free from drafts. Allow to rise for 2 hours, until doubled in bulk. Punch down, cover again, and allow to rise for an additional hour. Divide dough in half with a sharp knife and place in 2 well-greased loaf pans, 8½″×4½″×2½″. Cover and allow to rise for ½ hour in pans before baking.

Preheat oven to 375°.

With a sharp knife, make 3 diagonal cuts on top of each loaf, about ½-inch deep. Brush tops with beaten egg white and water. Lightly press 1 teaspoon mustard seeds into top of each loaf. Place a large baking pan of hot water on floor of oven. Bake loaves for about 50 minutes or until they sound hollow when tapped. For a very crusty bread, brush tops with cold water 3 or 4 times during baking. Remove from baking pans immediately when done to prevent sogginess. Transfer to cooling racks and allow to cool completely, right side up.

Makes 2 loaves.

Pie Pastry

1½ cups flour
8 tablespoons cold butter cut into ½-inch cubes
1 tablespoon sugar
2–3 tablespoons ice water

Put flour, butter, and sugar into container of a food processor. Start blending. Gradually add enough water so that dough can be gathered into a fairly cohesive ball. (If a food processor is not used, place flour and sugar in a mixing bowl. Add butter, and cut it in with 2 knives or a pastry blender until mixture looks like coarse cornmeal. Add water, stirring quickly with a fork.)

Gather dough into a ball. Flatten ball into a round disk 1-inch thick. Wrap dough in wax paper, and chill for 1 hour or less.

Makes pastry for one 8- to 9-inch pie.

Pumpkin Bread

2⅔ cups flour
3 cups sugar
2 teaspoons baking soda
2 teaspoons nutmeg
2 teaspoons cinnamon
1½ teaspoons salt
1½ teaspoons cloves
1 teaspoon allspice
4 eggs
1 cup oil
⅔ cup water
1 cup chopped nuts
1 16-ounce can pumpkin

Preheat oven to 325°.

Blend flour, sugar, soda, nutmeg, cinnamon, salt, cloves, and allspice. In another bowl, mix together eggs, oil, water, nuts, and pumpkin. Thoroughly mix dry ingredients into pumpkin mixture. Pour into 2 ungreased loaf pans. Bake for 1½ hours. Let set ½ hour before removing from pans.

Makes 2 loaves.

Whole-Wheat Tortillas

4 cups whole-wheat flour
1 teaspoon salt
4 tablespoons oil
1 cup water

Mix together flour and salt. Add oil, mixing it in with your fingers or a fork until mixture is homogeneous. Stir in water. Work dough in a bowl until it holds together easily. If dough continues to crumble, add a little water, 1 tablespoon at a time, until dough holds together.

Take dough out of bowl. Knead dough on a lightly floured surface until it is smooth and elastic, about 5 minutes. Divide dough into 20 equal pieces, and form each piece into a ball. Roll balls out on a well-floured surface into circles about 7 inches in diameter. Stack tortillas, and keep them covered to prevent drying out.

Heat a cast-iron skillet or other heavy griddle. Do not butter or oil pan. Cook tortillas one at a time for 1–2 minutes on each side. If they puff up, press down gently with a spatula. Tortillas are done when light brown spots show evenly on both sides.

Makes 20 tortillas.

Fruit Desserts

Glazed Bananas Peking

1½ cups flour
1 egg
3 cups water
4 medium bananas
1 cup sugar
Ice water

Put flour in a bowl, and make a well in center. Combine egg with 1 cup water, and pour into well, a little at a time. Combine egg with flour. Stir batter until smooth. Cut peeled bananas into bite-size pieces. Dip banana pieces into batter and fry in hot, deep oil at 375° until crisp and golden. Drain bananas on paper towels.

In a medium skillet, dissolve sugar in 2 cups water, brushing down any sugar that clings to sides of skillet. Cook syrup over moderately high heat until it reaches the hard-crack stage, or a candy thermometer registers 290°. Add bananas, coating them quickly with syrup, and serve immediately with a bowl of ice water for dipping.

Makes 4 servings.

Cherries Jubilee

Here's a dessert that's as synonymous with elegance as caviar or truffles. Actually, it's very simple to make, and since the best recipes always call for canned cherries, it can be served any time of the year.

1 can pitted black cherries
1 tablespoon sugar
1 tablespoon cornstarch
¼ cup warmed cognac
Vanilla ice cream

Drain cherries, reserving juice. Mix sugar with cornstarch. Add 1 cup reserved juice, a little at a time. Cook 3 minutes, stirring constantly. Add cherries, and pour cognac over top. Ignite cognac, and ladle sauce over vanilla ice cream.

Serves 6.

Mangoes and Sticky Rice (Mamuang Kao Nieo)

The fruits of Thailand have to be seen to be believed. The variety is endless: jackfruit (kanoon), coconut (ma-phrao), durien (Thailand's fruit of fruit), tamarind (ma-karm), guava (fa-rang), papaya (ma-la-gaw), longan (lam-yai), custard apple (noi-na); zalacca, rambuta, pomelo, Indian jujube, pineapple, banana, mimusops, grapes, and of course, mango.

For a dessert that can't be beaten—or even Thaid—here's the recipe for Mangoes and Sticky Rice, Thailand's most popular dessert.

1½ cups glutinous rice (sticky or sweet rice), soaked
   overnight and drained
2 cups water
1 cup "thick" canned coconut milk, boiled until reduced
   by ⅓
½ cup granulated sugar
½ teaspoon salt
5 ripe mangoes, peeled, halved, pitted, and each half
   cut into 4 transverse slices
4 tablespoons coconut "cream"

Cook rice in 2 cups water, simmering until most of water has evaporated. Pour thick coconut milk into a bowl, and stir in sugar and salt until dissolved. Add warm rice, and let stand for 30 minutes.

Arrange reassembled mango halves on a platter, and spoon sticky rice in heaps beside them. Spoon coconut cream over sticky rice. Serve immediately.

Serves 6.

Frozen Peach Dessert

Crust
1¼ cups graham cracker crumbs, plus crumbs for top
⅓ cup sugar
1 teaspoon cinnamon
⅓ cup butter, melted

Blend crumbs, sugar, and cinnamon. Mix melted butter into crumbs. Spread crumbs in a 1-quart shallow pan to make a bottom crust.

Filling
2 cups mashed fresh peaches (5–6 peaches)
1 tablespoon fresh lemon juice
1 cup sugar
½ pint heavy cream
Coconut

Drop peaches in boiling water, and let stand until skins come off easily. Peel, cut up in small pieces, and mash with a fork, or chop in blender. Sprinkle lemon juice on peaches. Mix in sugar. Whip cream until it is stiff, and fold into mashed peaches. Pour peach mixture onto crumb crust. Sprinkle reserved crumbs over top, and cover with foil. Freeze from 4–6 hours, or until firm.

Remove from freezer ½ hour before serving. Cut into squares. Keep in refrigerator until ready to serve. Sprinkle with coconut.

Serves 6 to 8.

Poached Pears with Ginger

Poached Pears
½ lemon
10 pears (ripe but still firm)
2 cups sugar
2 cups water
1 cup Sauterne or other white dessert wine
¼ cup grated or finely chopped fresh ginger (packed firm)

Ginger Cream
2 cups whipping cream
½ cup sugar
2 eggs, separated
1 teaspoon ground ginger
1 ounce Amaretto liqueur

Ginger Topping
2 cups poaching liquid from pears
¾ cup slivered almonds, toasted (optional garnish)

For pears: Squeeze lemon juice into large bowl of cold water. Peel pears; remove blossom end with small melon baller, but leave core and stem intact. Immediately plunge into water to retain color.

Combine sugar, water, wine, and ginger in large nonaluminum Dutch oven. Cover and bring to boil, stirring several times to make sure sugar is completely dissolved. Reduce heat and stand 5 pears upright in bottom of pan. Cover and poach (simmer) gently until pears are tender, about 30 minutes. Remove with slotted spoon and transfer to dish large enough to hold all pears in single layer. Poach remaining pears and add to dish. Strain all but 2 cups poaching syrup over pears. Let pears cool to room temperature, cover, and refrigerate overnight.

Combine ginger in sieve with 2 cups remaining syrup in 1½ to 2-quart saucepan, cover, and set aside for ginger topping.

For ginger cream: Combine cream with ¼ cup sugar in 2-quart saucepan. Heat until glossy film forms on top; do not boil. Let cool slightly.

Beat egg yolks with remaining ¼ cup sugar and ginger in large bowl until light and fluffy. Begin adding cream a few drops at a time; beat well, then gradually add remainder. Return mixture to saucepan and cook over medium heat until custard is thick enough to coat metal spoon. Remove from heat, and stir in liqueur. Let cool.

Beat egg whites until stiff but not dry. Stir about ⅓ of beaten whites into cooled yolk mixture to lighten custard. Gently fold in remainder. Cover and chill overnight.

For topping: Bring reserved poaching syrup to boil over medium-high heat. Reduce heat and simmer, shaking pan occasionally, until syrup is thickened, about 30 minutes. Keep warm in double boiler until ready to serve.

To serve: Place ginger cream in balloon wine goblets or glass dessert bowls. Top with a pear, drizzle with syrup, and sprinkle with almonds.

Makes 10 servings.

Pears and Ricotta

8 pears
1 cup sugar
4 tablespoons brandy
2 pounds Ricotta cheese
½ cup cocoa

Peel pears, cut each into 8 wedges, and remove core. Cook pears just covered in water with ½ cup sugar until tender, about 15 minutes. Remove pears. Boil cooking liquid until it is thick and syrupy, about 30 minutes. Cool. Stir in brandy, remaining sugar, Ricotta, and cocoa until smooth.

Place pears in dessert glasses. Spoon Ricotta mixture over pears. Chill until ready to serve.

Serves 8.

Raspberry Whip

3 egg whites
½ cup sugar
1 cup raspberries
Fresh mint

Beat egg whites until stiff, gradually adding sugar. Purée raspberries in a blender or food processor, and fold into egg white mixture. Chill before serving. Serve in dessert glasses, each garnished with a sprig of fresh mint.

Serves 4 to 6.

Flaming Rhubarb

½ cup dry red wine
1 pound fresh rhubarb, trimmed and coarsely chopped (or 12-ounce package frozen rhubarb)
½–¾ cup sugar
⅛ teaspoon salt
1 tablespoon cornstarch
2 pints rum raisin ice cream
6 ounces brandy (optional)

In a chafing dish, or in a saucepan on the stove, bring wine to boil. Add rhubarb and simmer until just tender, about 5 minutes. Blend together sugar, salt, and cornstarch, and mix into rhubarb-wine thoroughly. Cook, stirring constantly, until sauce is thickened and clear.

Serve each person rum raisin ice cream topped with rhubarb sauce. If desired, heat brandy until fumes just rise, then pour over rhubarb sauce in chafing dish. Set alight and ladle this sauce (flaming or not) over ice cream.

Serves 6.

Cakes

Apple Cake

3 large, firm tart apples (Granny Smith)
⅓ cup rum
4 eggs
2 cups sugar
Grated rind of 1 lemon
3½ cups flour
2 teaspoons baking powder
Butter and flour for pan

Preheat oven to 350°.

Peel and core apples. Very thinly slice apples into a bowl, and pour rum over them. Beat eggs with 1½ cups sugar until thick and light. Beat in lemon rind. Sift together flour and baking powder; stir gradually into batter. Butter and flour a 7" × 11" × 1" baking pan. Turn dough into pan and smooth out. Place apple slices in orderly rows on top of dough. Sprinkle with remaining sugar. Bake for 35–40 minutes. Serve at room temperature.

Serves 6.

Baklava

Even though most of these recipes are not "hassle-free," making fillo (or phyllo) dough is really too much to do at home. Truly. It's so readily available all over the country now in

1-pound packages (often labeled "strudel dough") that I recommend you buy it and use it according to package directions.

Basic Syrup
2 cups sugar
1½ cups water
Rind of ½ lemon, finely cut
5 whole cloves
2 cinnamon sticks
1 cup honey
4 tablespoons lemon juice
2 tablespoons rum or brandy
1 tablespoon rum flavoring (optional)

In a saucepan, combine sugar, water, lemon rind, cloves, and
cinnamon sticks. Bring to a boil and cook until syrup thickens
slightly. Remove from flame and add honey, lemon juice, li-
quor, and flavoring. Store in a cool place but not in the refrigerator where it might crystallize. This syrup will keep well, at least
1 month.

Makes 4 cups

Baklava
1 pound walnuts, coarsely chopped
½ pound blanched almonds, finely chopped
½ cup sugar
2 teaspoons cinnamon
Fillo pastry
1½ pounds butter, melted
4 cups Basic Syrup

Preheat oven to 325°.

Combine chopped walnuts and almonds. Add sugar and cinnamon and mix together thoroughly. Divide mixture in 4 equal
parts. Line bottom of a 13″ × 9″ × 2″ baking pan with 10 layers of
fillo, brushing each sheet with butter before applying the next.
Sprinkle a quarter of nut mixture over entire layer. Add 6 more
layers of fillo, brushing each layer with butter, and cover with a
quarter of mixture. Repeat twice, then cover with 10 layers of
fillo.

Cut Baklava in 2-inch diamond-shaped pieces, being sure to cut through to bottom of pan. Pour remaining melted butter over Baklava. Bake for 1 hour, covering with foil for last 20 minutes to keep pastry from becoming too brown. Remove from oven. Slowly pour 2 cups of cool Basic Syrup over hot Baklava. One hour later, pour remaining 2 cups of Basic Syrup over Baklava. Store in same pan in a cool place, but not in refrigerator. Best served the following day but will keep up to 10 days.

Makes 40 small pieces.

Ginger Cheesecake

Butter for pan
½ cup crushed ginger snaps
½ cup crushed chocolate wafers
⅓ cup butter, melted
2 pounds cream cheese, at room temperature
½ cup heavy cream
4 eggs
1½ cups sugar
1 teaspoon vanilla extract
2 tablespoons freshly grated ginger
1 cup finely chopped candied ginger

Preheat oven to 300°.

Butter inside of a metal cheesecake pan 8 inches wide and 3 inches deep. Combine crushed ginger snaps and chocolate wafers, and mix with melted butter. Press crumbs into bottom and halfway up sides of pan.

Place cream cheese, heavy cream, eggs, sugar, vanilla, and grated ginger into bowl of an electric mixer. Beat ingredients until thoroughly blended and quite smooth. Mix in chopped ginger. Pour batter into prepared pan, and shake gently to level mixture. Set pan into a slightly larger pan, and pour boiling water into larger pan to a depth of 2 inches. Do not let edges of pans touch. Bake for 1 hour 40 minutes. Turn off oven, and let cake sit in oven 1 hour longer.

Lift cake out of water bath and place on a rack to cool at least 2 hours before unmolding.

To unmold, place a round cake plate over cheesecake and carefully turn both upside down. Repeat, inverting cake onto serving plate.

Serves 12 to 14.

Sticky Gingerbread

8 ounces butter
1¼ cups dark brown sugar
1¼ cups molasses
2 eggs, beaten
2¼ cups flour
2 teaspoons ground ginger
1 tablespoon cinnamon
3 tablespoons warm milk
1 teaspoon baking soda
Fresh whipped cream

Preheat oven to 300°.

Melt butter, sugar, and molasses over low heat in a medium saucepan. Add eggs, flour, ginger, and cinnamon, and mix well. Add milk and baking soda. Remove mixture from heat, and pour into a well-greased 9-inch cake pan. Bake for 40 minutes.

Cut gingerbread into small squares. Allow gingerbread to cool. Serve topped with a dollop of fresh whipped cream.

Serves 6 to 8.

Hazelnut Cake

Butter and flour for pan
3 eggs
1 cup sugar
Grated rind of 1 lemon
8 tablespoons butter (1 stick), cut into small pieces
1 teaspoon baking powder
1⅔ cup flour
1¼ cups hazelnuts, ground fine in blender
1 tablespoon olive oil
½ cup milk

Preheat oven to 350°.

Butter and flour an 8-inch springform baking pan. Beat together eggs and sugar until very thick. Beat in lemon rind and butter, piece by piece. Sift together baking powder and flour. Fold gently into batter. Add hazelnuts, olive oil, and ⅓ cup of milk, mixing well to make a medium-soft batter. If necessary, add another spoonful or two of milk. Turn into springform pan. Bake for 45–60 minutes, or until cake shrinks from sides of pan and tests done.

Makes one 8-inch cake.

Lemon Roll

1 cup (2 sticks) butter
⅔ cup sugar
¼ cup water
¼ cup lemon juice
¼ teaspoon cream of tartar
8 egg yolks
1½ teaspoons grated lemon rind
4 egg whites
¼ cup sugar
¼ cup sifted flour

¼ cup cornstarch
½ teaspoon vanilla
½ teaspoon grated lemon rind
Confectioners' sugar

In a heavy enamel saucepan, combine butter, ⅔ cup sugar, water, lemon juice, cream of tartar, and 4 egg yolks. Stir mixture over low heat until it is thickened and coats spoon. Remove pan from heat and add grated lemon rind. Pour mixture into a bowl and let cool. Cover bowl with a round of buttered wax paper. Chill for several hours, or until firm.

Preheat oven to 400°.

Butter a jelly roll pan, 11" × 16", line pan with wax paper, and butter the paper. In a bowl, beat egg whites until frothy. Add ¼ cup sugar 1 tablespoon at a time. Beat whites until stiff. In another bowl, beat 4 remaining egg yolks until they are light. Fold a quarter of the egg-white mixture into the yolks gently but thoroughly. Pour yolk mixture onto remaining whites, and sift flour and cornstarch over top. Fold mixtures together gently, adding vanilla and lemon rind, until there are no traces of white. Turn batter into prepared pan, and spread it evenly with a metal spatula. Bake in hot oven for 10 minutes or until lightly browned. Loosen wax paper from sides of pan, and invert cake onto a baking sheet covered with a sheet of wax paper sprinkled with sifted confectioners' sugar.

Let cake cool. Peel off paper from top. Spread cake with filling. Roll up filled cake tightly, lifting it with wax paper. Finish with seam side down. Dust cake roll with sifted confectioners' sugar.

Serves 6 to 8.

Pies

Chocolate Pie in Meringue Crust

Meringue Crust
2 egg whites
⅛ teaspoon salt
⅛ teaspoon cream of tartar
½ cup sugar
½ cup chopped walnuts or pecans
½ teaspoon vanilla extract

Preheat oven to 300°.

Combine egg whites, salt, and cream of tartar in a mixing bowl. Beat until foamy. Add sugar, 2 tablespoons at a time, beating after each addition until sugar is blended into egg whites. Continue beating until mixture stands in very stiff peaks. Fold in nuts and vanilla, and blend.

Spoon meringue mixture into a lightly greased 8-inch pie pan. Spread meringue over bottom of pan and about 1 inch up the sides, but not over the rim. Bake 50–55 minutes. Cool.

Chocolate Pie
1 package (4 ounces) sweet baking chocolate
3 tablespoons water
1 teaspoon vanilla extract
1 cup heavy cream
Baked Meringue Crust

Place chocolate and water in a saucepan over low heat. Stir until chocolate has melted. Cool.

Add vanilla to chocolate. Whip cream to a soft consistency. Fold chocolate mixture into whipped cream, and pile into cooled meringue shell. Chill before serving.

Serves 6.

Note: If desired, you can omit the Meringue Crust and serve the chocolate filling as a pudding.

Chocolate Mint Pie

They all laughed when I mentioned this recipe. They'll probably laugh when *you* mention it—so don't tell them there's tofu in it, and get the last laugh as they lick their plates clean.

Crust
1½ cups fine graham cracker crumbs
6 tablespoons melted butter
½ teaspoon brown sugar
1 teaspoon cinnamon

Filling
½ cup honey
½ cup cocoa (or carob powder)
4 teaspoons vanilla extract
1 teaspoon peppermint extract
½ teaspoon cinnamon (optional)
1½ pounds tofu (pressed dry)
½ teaspoon agar-agar powder
½ cup water

Preheat oven to 350°.

Combine crust ingredients and mix well. Press mixture into a 9-inch pie pan. Prebake for 10 minutes.

Combine all filling ingredients, except tofu, agar-agar, and water, in a blender or food processor. Add tofu, piece by piece, and blend until smooth.

Add agar-agar powder to water, and bring to a boil, stirring to dissolve. Let simmer for 5 minutes, stirring occasionally, then add immediately to filling mixture, and blend until very smooth. Pour into pie shell and chill for 1–2 hours, until firm.

Makes one 9-inch pie.

Spanish Lime Pie

Crust
1¼ cups graham cracker crumbs
1 tablespoon sugar
1 teaspoon cinnamon
6 tablespoons butter, melted

Preheat oven to 375°.

Mix graham cracker crumbs with sugar and cinnamon. Add melted butter. Stir with a rubber spatula, pressing mixture against sides of bowl, until completely mixed. Press mixture into a 9-inch pie plate. (Crust will look crumbly in bowl but will hold together in pie plate.)

Bake for 8–10 minutes. Remove and allow to cool to room temperature.

Filling
Finely grated rind of 2 limes
1 cup lime juice
4 eggs, separated
2 15-ounce cans sweetened condensed milk
Pinch of salt

Mix lime rind and juice. In a large mixing bowl, stir yolks lightly with a small wire whisk or a fork just to mix. Gradually mix in condensed milk. Very gradually add rind and juice, stirring until smooth. Add salt to whites, and beat until whites hold a point, or are stiff but not dry. In 2 or 3 steps, fold whites into yolk mixture.

The crust will not hold all the filling. Pour in as much as crust will hold without any running over. Reserve balance at room temperature. Freeze filled crust for about 20 minutes, until semifirm. Pour balance of filling on top, mounding it high in center. Return to freezer immediately. Freeze for 4–5 hours, until firm. (May be frozen overnight or longer.) Let stand at room temperature 5–10 minutes before serving.

Serves 8.

Custards, Puddings, and Ices

Chilled Apricot-Orange Crème

½ pound dried apricots
1 medium orange
½ cup sugar
¼ cup chopped walnuts
¼ cup orange-flavored liqueur
½ pint heavy cream, whipped
1 square bitter chocolate

Place apricots in a saucepan, and cover with cold water. Allow to soak for several hours until soft. Chop entire orange, pulp and rind, in a blender or food processor. Add orange and sugar to apricots. Cook apricot-orange mixture over very low heat until tender and most liquid is absorbed—about 10–15 minutes. Remove from heat.

When mixture is cool, blend in a blender or food processor. Remove to a mixing bowl, and stir in nuts and liqueur. Fold in whipped cream. Transfer to individual serving bowls, sprinkle each with grated chocolate, and serve.

Serves 6.

Blueberry Pudding

2 cups flour, plus 2 tablespoons flour
¼ cup sugar
2 teaspoons baking powder

½ teaspoon salt
½ teaspoon nutmeg
6 tablespoons cold butter (¾ stick)
1 egg, lightly beaten
¼ cup honey
1 tablespoon lemon juice
1 cup milk
1½ cups blueberries
Butter for mold
1 cup warmed honey

Into a bowl, sift together flour, sugar, 1½ teaspoons baking powder, salt, and nutmeg. Blend in butter, cut into bits. In a small bowl, combine egg, honey, and lemon juice. Make a well in center of flour mixture, and pour in egg mixture and milk. Blend mixture with a fork. In another bowl, toss 2 tablespoons flour and ½ teaspoon baking powder with blueberries. Fold berries into batter.

Coat with sugar a well-buttered 1½-quart steamed-pudding mold and its lid. Transfer batter to mold. Cover mold first with a buttered round of wax paper and then with lid. Place mold on a rack in a kettle. Add enough boiling water to reach two-thirds of the way up sides of mold. Return water to a boil, cover kettle, and steam pudding over very low heat for 2 hours. Remove mold from kettle. Remove lid and paper. Let pudding cool for 30 minutes, then unmold onto a serving dish. Serve pudding with honey.

Serves 6 to 8.

Bread Custard (Coach House)

¾ cup butter, melted
12 slices French bread cut ½-inch thick, crusts trimmed
5 whole eggs
4 egg yolks
1 cup sugar
Pinch nutmeg

⅛ teaspoon salt
1 quart milk
1 cup heavy cream
1 teaspoon vanilla extract
Confectioners' sugar

Preheat oven to 375°.

Butter 1 side of each slice of bread, and set aside.

Beat together eggs, yolks, sugar, nutmeg, and salt in a large bowl until thoroughly combined. Set aside. Arrange slices of bread, buttered side up, in a 2-quart soufflé dish or ovenproof bowl, and strain custard mixture over them. Pour boiling water into a roasting pan to a depth of about 1 inch. Set soufflé dish in pan, place in oven, and bake about 45 minutes, or until a knife inserted in center comes out clean. Remove custard dish from pan, and sprinkle generously with confectioners' sugar. Put pudding under broiler for a few minutes, watching carefully so that bread is just glazed and not burned.

At the Coach House, Bread Custard is served at room temperature, with a purée of fresh raspberries.

Serves 8 to 10.

Flan (Caramel Custard)

1¼ cups sugar
⅛ teaspoon salt
2 teaspoons vanilla extract
7 large eggs
½ cup cold milk
4 cups hot milk

Preheat oven to 325°.

Cook, stirring, ¾ cup sugar in a small saucepan over medium heat until it is melted and light amber in color. Pour into a 1½-quart casserole, turning dish to coat entire bottom and as much of sides as possible. (If casserole is very cold, place in pan of hot water to warm. This prevents caramel from hardening before bottom and sides are coated.)

Combine salt, vanilla, and remaining sugar. Mix well. Add eggs, and beat lightly with a rotary beater. Stir in cold milk, then add hot milk. Mix well. Pour custard into caramel-coated casserole. Set in a pan of hot water. Bake for 1 hour 20 minutes.

Remove from oven and cool. Then chill. Just before serving, turn flan out into a shallow bowl or a slightly cupped serving plate about 2 inches larger than flan. Slice and serve.

Serves 12.

Chocolate Mousse

1 cup milk
1 cup water
¼ cup sugar
4 ounces bittersweet chocolate
4 eggs, separated
½ cup heavy cream
1 teaspoon vanilla extract
2 tablespoons Grand Marnier liqueur
1 teaspoon freshly grated orange peel

In saucepan, combine milk, water, sugar, and chocolate, and bring to a slow boil, stirring often.

In a bowl, beat egg yolks, and combine with a quarter of the milk mixture. Return egg-yolk mixture to saucepan. Cook over low heat until mixture begins to thicken. Place saucepan in a bowl of ice to cool.

In another bowl, beat cream until firm. In a third bowl, beat egg whites until stiff. Fold whites into whipped cream. Fold in remaining ingredients.

Fold cream mixture into chocolate mixture. Spoon into 8 dessert cups. Chill before serving.

Serves 8.

Chocolate Sorbet

1¾ cups unsweetened cocoa
1 cup sugar
⅛ teaspoon salt
3½ cups nonfat milk
Vanilla bean

Combine cocoa, sugar, and salt in medium saucepan, and mix well. Gradually stir in milk. Split vanilla bean, scrape out seeds, and add bean to pan. Place over medium heat and bring just to boil, stirring constantly. Reduce heat and simmer, stirring constantly, 5 minutes. Let cool, then remove vanilla bean. Pour into shallow pan and freeze.

Spoon into a food processor, and mix until smooth. Return to freezer, if needed, or scoop into dishes and serve.

Makes about ten ½-cup servings.

Cocada (Coconut Pudding)

1 cup sugar
1 cup water
2 large cinnamon sticks
1 3½-ounce package shredded coconut
1 quart milk
3 egg yolks, well beaten
¼ cup cold milk
Butter for platter
½ cup toasted almonds, chopped

Combine sugar, water, and cinnamon sticks, and boil for 10 minutes. Remove cinnamon. Add coconut, and cook until coconut absorbs syrup and is dry. Bring 1 quart milk to a boil over low heat in a deep saucepan. Add coconut, and cook until of custard consistency, stirring frequently to prevent sticking. Mix yolks with ¼ cup cold milk. Add yolk mixture to pudding, and continue cooking slowly, stirring constantly until thick. Pour pudding onto a buttered platter, and allow to cool before refrigerating. Serve garnished with toasted almonds.

Serves 6 to 8.

Grapefruit Ice

2 cups sugar
2 cups water
Grated rind of 1 grapefruit
4 cups freshly squeezed grapefruit juice
⅓ cup lemon juice

Combine sugar and water in a saucepan and bring to a boil. Lower flame and simmer for 5 minutes. Remove from flame and allow to cool. Add grapefruit rind and juice and lemon juice. Mix until smooth using a wooden spoon, and freeze.

Remove from freezer. Put frozen mixture into a food processor or blender and blend until smooth. Place in individual dessert glasses and return to freezer until ready to serve.

Serves 8 to 10.

Frozen Honey Mousse

4 eggs, separated, plus 2 egg yolks
1½ cups honey
2 cups heavy cream
Pinch of salt

In top of a double boiler, off the heat, beat 6 egg yolks briefly with a small wire whisk. Beat in honey. Cook over simmering water on moderate heat, stirring constantly, for about 10 minutes.

Remove mixture from heat, and place top of double boiler into a bowl of ice and water. Keep stirring until mixture is cool. Remove from ice water and set aside.

In a chilled bowl, whip cream until it holds a soft shape. In another bowl, beat egg whites with a pinch of salt until they hold a definite shape, but are not dry.

Gradually fold about half the honey mixture into the whites. Gradually fold other half of honey mixture into whipped cream. In a large bowl, gently fold the two together. Turn mousse into a covered icebox container, or a 10- to 12-cup serving bowl, or 8 to 10 large wineglasses, leaving a bit of room at the top. Cover with plastic wrap or aluminum foil, and freeze until firm.

Serves 8 to 10.

Indian Pudding

Butter for dish
2 eggs
¾ cup molasses
⅓ cup firmly packed dark brown sugar
1 teaspoon ground cinnamon
1 teaspoon ground ginger
½ teaspoon salt
¼ teaspoon baking soda
4 cups milk
⅔ cup yellow cornmeal
3 tablespoons unsalted butter
Vanilla ice cream

Preheat oven to 350° F. Butter deep (preferably oval) 1½-quart baking dish.

Combine eggs, molasses, sugar, cinnamon, ginger, salt, baking soda, and 2½ cups milk in deep saucepan. Whisk until blended. Whisk in cornmeal. Cook over medium heat, stirring constantly, until mixture bubbles and becomes stiff. Remove from heat, add butter and remaining 1½ cups milk, and stir until smooth.

Turn into baking dish. Bake until pudding is still slightly soft in center, about 1¼ hours (pudding will continue to firm as it cools). Serve warm wtih ice cream.

Serves 6.

Granita di Limone (Lemon Ice)

8 cups crushed ice
Juice of 8 lemons
4 tablespoons sugar
Lemon slices

Fill sherbet glasses with crushed ice. Place in freezer until ready to serve. Mix lemon juice and sugar to taste. Stir until sugar is dissolved. Pour over ice. Serve at once, garnished with lemon slices.

Serves 8.

Lemon Soufflé

Butter and sugar for dish
½ cup sugar
½ cup butter, at room temperature
6 eggs, separated
Juice of 1 lemon
¼ teaspoon salt
Grated rind of 1 lemon

Prepare a soufflé dish by rubbing inside with butter, then sprinkle with enough sugar to coat well. Shake out excess sugar, and chill the dish until ready to use.

Preheat oven to 325°.

Combine sugar, butter, egg yolks, lemon juice, and salt in a heavy-bottomed saucepan. Place pan over hot water. Beat until mixture has the consistency of Mornay sauce. Stir in lemon rind and let stand. Beat egg whites until stiff. Stir half the whites into lemon mixture. Fold remaining whites into mixture. Pour mixture into prepared soufflé dish, and bake 35–45 minutes. Serve immediately.

Serves 6.

Peanut Butter Sauce for Ice Cream

1 cup sugar
1 tablespoon light corn syrup
⅛ teaspoon salt
¾ cup milk
2 tablespoons butter
⅓ cup smooth peanut butter
½ teaspoon vanilla extract

In a 6- to 8-cup heavy saucepan, mix sugar, corn syrup, salt, and milk. Stir over moderate heat until mixture comes to a boil. Adjust heat so that sauce boils gently. Boil without stirring for 30–40 minutes, until sauce caramelizes to a light golden color. Remove sauce from heat. Add butter and peanut butter. Stir briskly with a small whisk until smooth. Stir in vanilla.

Serve warm over ice cream. Sauce may be kept warm, or reheated in a small double boiler over hot water on moderate heat, stirring occasionally.

Makes 1¼ cups.

Pumpkin Pudding

⅔ cup sugar
1 tablespoon flour
½ teaspoon salt
1 teaspoon ginger
1 teaspoon cinnamon
¼ teaspoon nutmeg
⅛ teaspoon cloves
⅓ cup molasses
1 1-pound can pumpkin
3 eggs, separated
1 cup heavy cream

Preheat oven to 350°.

Mix together ⅓ cup sugar, flour, salt, ginger, cinnamon, nutmeg, and cloves. Add molasses, pumpkin, and egg yolks. Mix well. Stir in cream. Pour into a 1½-quart baking dish or casserole. Bake for 40–45 minutes, or until knife inserted in center comes out clean.

Beat egg whites until stiff but not dry. Gradually add remaining ⅓ cup sugar, and beat until very stiff. Spoon meringue around edge of baking dish, and place a spoonful of meringue in center. Return to oven and bake about 10 minutes more or until meringue is lightly browned.

Serves 6 to 8.

The Final Course

Well, there it is. The feast is over.

I, frankly, am totally and completely sated. As a cook, I have no shame in admitting that it really makes me feel good to see a dish come out of the oven, or off the top of the stove, and be just exactly what I wanted it to be both for myself and for my guests.

I feel even better when a book comes out of the typewriter—

or off the top of my head—and succeeds beyond my expectations. Well . . . that's not exactly true. This *is* the book I set out to write, so I suppose I shouldn't be surprised. . . . But again, it's like cooking—no matter how much confidence you have, no matter how many times you've done it before, it's a happy and glorious moment when things turn out exactly as you'd hoped.

   Bon appétit!

Index